A Beginners Guide to Collecting

Second Edition, 2010

John Ainsley B.A., B.Ed., Eng. Tech., M.I.I.E.

A Beginners Guide to Collecting

Second Edition, 2010

Author: John Ainsley

First published in Great Britain in 2009 by
Antiques Information Services Ltd. Wallsend House,
P O Box 93, Broadstairs, Kent CT10 3YR
Telephone: 01843 862069
Fax: 01843 862014
E-mail: enquiries@antiques-info.co.uk

Further details about the Publishers may be found on our website at
www.antiques-info.co.uk

ISBN: 978-0-9546479-6-4
Whilst every care has been exercised in the compilation of this guide,
neither the Editor nor Publishers accept any liability for any financial
or other loss incurred by reliance placed on the information contained
in *A Beginners Guide to Collecting*.

Printed in the United Kingdom
by Cromwell Press Group, Trowbridge, Wiltshire

Contents

Introduction

Since completing this work I have looked far and wide on the Web and to my knowledge no one has ever tackled the subject of offering general information and advice on collecting itself, that is in the 'nounal' sense of the word. Always the word 'collecting' has been used in the 'verbal' sense and always the book or the website or the paper is related to a particular area of collecting. I have come across beginners' guides to collecting military medals, on book collecting itself, on collecting autographs and collecting coins and first day covers and postcards and teddy bears, art and fishing tackle and railwayana and stamps and clocks and bakelite and maps *et al*, but never collecting *per se*, that is, in its intrinsic sense and with respect to the inherent nature of collecting. Where angels fear to tread? Maybe, and perhaps there will be paragraphs in these pages which might make certain people uneasy, but in general most will recognise that these pages applaud almost every aspect of the world of collecting and if on occasions, if I draw a little too much attention to certain dubious practices, it is never more than a hint! Rather it is to the commercial world outside of collecting that I concentrate my most scathing comments and in particular I will point up now the almost universally unethical practices of much of the financial services sector of the UK, who for the most part seem able to always and ever ride out the continuing condemnations! We have all been there and I relate some of my own experiences.

However let us begin at the beginning. **Chapter I** sets out a philosophy for collecting. This is deliberately controversial. I challenge what I consider the absurd notions peddled by some media experts, that collecting is, and shouldn't be anything other than a pleasure and that any realised investment is a bonus. Rather I place the emphasis on the importance of always ensuring that collectors try to make shrewd and prudent purchases, with investment firmly in mind. In short I lean a little to one side of the 'serendipity versus investment' debate. Furthermore I argue that collectors should try not to waste money always buying from the lower end of the market and should slap their own wrists long before they end up with a house full of affectionate junk that they cannot move on, except to a charity shop. This argument may be summarised as the 'commonplace versus the worthwhile' debate. More importantly I argue for the notion of the whole home as an investment arena, that is, for generalising as well as specialising, and I use statistics to back up my argument in what I might summarise as the 'new versus old' debate.

In **Chapter II**, I examine the world of information and knowledge and link study to successful dealing and collecting. I look at collectors' clubs, courses on antiques, the web as a source of information, and in particular the world of books and the importance of some and the irrelevance of most! I take a look at television and its successes and failures and in particular how it continues to pull the wool over our eyes. Television is I conclude in the main a source of entertainment with the vast majority of its programmes on antiques and collecting reduced to absurd game shows. In respect of showing how the antiques and collecting market works, they are frequently irresponsible and misleading. Only rarely are television programmes on antiques and collecting educational.

In **Chapter III** I look at the market in general and theorise about the 'fallacy of the shady market' in relation to the general public distrust in the industry and promote the notion of the 'fallacy of the bargain' because the notion of a bargain in itself is much peddled by so called media experts, with their absurd notions of 'what's hot and what's not'. I look at the nature of the antiques market in general. This study examines the macro market as well as the micro market and exposes further fallacies about the industry. Here I look at some of the pitfalls in the market and at labelling and invoices in relation to misleading content or omissions and how beginners can protect themselves by relating the buying situation to potential risk. Comparisons are made with the market outside of the world of antiques and collecting, particularly the food industry and the financial services sector.

In **Chapters IV, V** and **VI** I examine the nature and the history of the fairs market, the auctions market and the retail scene. These chapters deal with, for example the old **Shops Act, 1951**, the **Sunday Trading Act, 1994**, and the effects of the uniform business rate, The national parking meter scheme and out of town shopping centres. **Chapter VI** begins with *The Old Curiosity Shop* by Charles Dickens and looks at the history of curiosity shops and the beginnings of 'antiques shops' and 'antiques centres'. There is much to applaud. I give it two cheers out of three and nine out of ten for for honesty, integrity, commitment and effort. The wider market is a far greater challenge and a far greater danger to our pockets and our pride then we are ever likely to find within the antiques industry.

Chapter VII looks at buying on the World Wide Web as a shopping experience and I explain and provide examples of its critical importance to collectors and dealers. I explain how we can cut out the miles and the hours of driving of yesteryear and search the longest high street in history, from our own homes. Most of this chapter is devoted to the law and the internet and in particular to internet auction sites. I discuss tricks of the trade, site protection schemes, dispute resolution schemes and payment protection schemes and how they may compromise your rights under **Section 75** of the **Consumer Credit Act**. Full details are provided on consumer websites and telephone numbers such as **Consumer Direct**, the **Office of Fair Trading** and local **Trading Standards**, as well as the police.

Chapter I

A Philosophy for Collectors

Collecting, above all else we are told, is a pastime and a great source of pleasure to millions of people worldwide. As an outdoor, as well as an indoor activity I am also certain that it promotes our health and our welfare. For many of us we also see ourselves as the temporary custodians of much of our heritage, one day to be sold on or relinquished and passed down to others, perhaps even younger family members. At times it can be exhilarating and at other times frustrating, but it is never dull and only occasionally disappointing. An interest in collecting may appear at an early age or it may develop later in life. As taste matures or as tastes change so may change what is collected, or the quality of the collection. The boy of yesterday may have collected war shrapnel or cigarette cards or imperial coinage, the man of today Georgian drinking glasses or Lowry prints, thus providing a personal and perhaps with the latter, a sentimental link to childhood. Tomorrow's man may refine these collections or seek instead only silver of superb quality and rarity, or antiques created from the designs of Dr Christopher Dresser.

Whilst collecting is many things those who sing its praises praise the paradoxical, the unexpected, the unplanned excitement of collecting. Certainly serendipity, the art of making happy and unexpected discoveries by chance, is often around the corner, but collecting may also be much more than the occasional bliss derived from accidental encounters. Indeed if we are to philosophise about our subject we must recognise that prudent collecting is also an intellectual pursuit and for many of us there has to be aims as well as objectives, stepping stones beyond the simplified and hackneyed notion of collecting merely for pleasure. Observe other collectors as they pursue their 'pleasure'. Watch television programmes about collecting. Scan the faces of the crowds at fairs. Better still study the prospective buyers at an auction. Listen to the conversations all around you in any of the different areas of the market and you will hear that collecting is also about investing and money matters are central to the dealing. Very few people I believe buy only for pleasure. For many they feel, and rightly so, that they are also buying as an investment. Experts never tire of telling us that we should consider our collections as amusements only and that if they prove also to be a good investment then we should think of this as a bonus. Such a generalisation is absurd and can at most only apply to a very restricted group of people. I say follow your star as you will but always try to make prudent, sensible, and if possible shrewd purchases. And if you make a mistake, make sure you learn from it so that you never make the same mistake too often. This way you get a bonus either way! Study your chosen field. Study every aspect of the market and your collection and your investment should prosper. If it doesn't then you will have enjoyed the experience and the collection becomes the bonus, not the investment.

Make only worthwhile purchases

No one could favour collecting more so than yours truly and yet my next piece of advice, if you are to make only shrewd and sensible purchases is actually to avoid buying on most occasions! In the general secondhand and even antiques market most of the goods readily available are, by their nature, commonplace. Collecting such objects, no matter how old, is a worthless and pointless pursuit. Collecting should be a worthwhile activity, intelligently pursuing worthwhile aims. Let us examine the most obvious mistake. If you are quickly able to form a collection then you should be asking yourself some very serious questions. It is easy to fill every available space in your home with old bottles and believe me people do. It is also easy to fill every available space with modern pottery or porcelain figurines, which are turned out in their millions by all of the well known manufacturers. It is easy to fill every available space in your home with dolls or cranberry or crinoline ladies, but if you can then it is time to stop. Collecting for its own sake is a pointless waste of time and money. There may be much serendipity on which to look back but there can be little sense in such a collection. To use a hackneyed phrase, I wish I had a pound for every collector who has approached me for advice on how to dispose of such a collection. I cannot help them move what often amounts to a veritable mountain of what is no more than affectionate junk that can be had almost anywhere. The ringing of the hands now should have been preceded in the beginning by the slapping of wrists. Auctions aren't interested in such collections, dealers will only pick out any cherries and if you take such a collection to a fair and try to sell it yourself you will bring most of it home again, except of course for the cherries, provided you have the knowledge to price them sensibly. Try never to buy from the bottom end of the market unless you find a serious bargain. The general advice is to buy the best you can afford. The trouble with this advice is that I have never heard it qualified or quantified. It seems that most of the experts seem to believe that everyone is stuck at a level depending on their disposable income. I profoundly disagree. By restricting your purchases and by buying the best you can afford you are already raising the status and hopefully the value of your collection. You are already affording the better antiques and collectibles by not frittering your income away with common or garden goods. You can go further. In general, and ignoring the volatility of fashionable collecting, it is mainly the case that it is the higher end of the market that prospers whilst the middle and certainly the lower end stagnates. This has been the case in recent times in almost every category of antiques. If your interest is the twentieth century then the market may lack the stability found in traditional antiques. The media are much to blame for the hyperbole with their absurd notions of 'what's hot' and as a result many fingers have been burnt! Therefore provided you are buying in the long term tried and tested market then it makes sense to restrict your collection to the worthwhile.

Move up market by saving

This may even mean saving your money until the right investments come along. You can usually forget spending, say in the £5 to £10 range. Save your money until you have say, £50, or better still, save the £50s until you have £500 or whatever you need at your level of the market and in your area of collecting. If you know your subject and you have studied the market you will know what you are targeting and how much you are going to have to pay to achieve the collection you seek.

I have talked about the worthwhile so much that it is only reasonable that I explain my meaning. I believe that the worthwhile connotates to fine and perhaps even exceptional quality. Such art and antiques are by their nature rare because in most cases much time and expertise has gone into their production, unless they are the almost instant work of genius and fame, such as an Old Master sketch, in which case they are in themselves rare and desirable. In any event the production of such goods would have been restricted to a wealthier clientele or even have been made to order. But rarity in itself is also highly valued. Take English delft, and note that I spell it with a small 'd.' Made in large quantities between say, 1600 and 1750, today the rarer pieces can command tens of thousands of pounds and even at the lower end of the market you are going to have to pay anything from a £100 upwards for what was, in its day no more than utilitarian ware. But there is also rarity achieved by limited production. Bronzes may come into this category as well as some Doulton figures but beware the latter as collecting Doulton is a modern phenomenon, a fashion craze, and there is no certainty in the future for this highly volatile area of the twentieth century ceramics market. Don't either confuse limited editions with rarity, another finger-burning area. These are usually the new goods side of the collecting arena and apart from the occasional investment success, such as the Royal Crown Derby Siamese Cat paperweight, is not favoured for its investment potential. By the way cats are one of the more popular perennials in the world of collecting. In any event if you are reading this book in the first place then you are unlikely to be investing in new limited editions although going by letters I receive as Editor of *Antiques Info* some mistakingly feel that they are sitting on potentially profit making collections.

Specialising

Let us now reconsider our position in respect of the advice I have given so far in the narrow field of specialising as opposed to the broader background of life and the market in general. Let us first sing the praises of specialising, which for most collectors will come naturally. We are all of us to a great extent ruled by our hearts. We are going to collect what we like and we are going to enjoy the experience. But hopefully we are also going to be strongly influenced by our heads. Years of study and experience has the potential in the longer term to make us experts in our chosen field. In time you may become a master of your subject and enjoy a distinct advantage over other mortals. You will be blessed with the Midas touch and a taste for the rare and the extraordinary. You will absorb every rumour that is whispered in your field and see at great distances. All of your primary senses will be so in tune that you will develop a second sense. You may go on to enjoy also the spin-offs and the rewards of knowledge. You may write books or make guest appearances or even become a dealer in your chosen subject. Or you may just enjoy and profit from your hobby. Tens of thousands of us nationwide have, over the years, created fine collections but probably only 10% of these have taken the notion of collecting and investing much further. In this sense I think that the majority have failed!

What I have written up to now is important and I sincerely hope useful to those who are collectors or who are in the process of beginning to think of forming a collection. But I ask much more. I ask readers to consider broader implications related to collecting and investing than I have discussed up to now. I ask readers to give much greater weight to what I am now about to write!

Widening your horizons and investments

Buying across a broad household range is more important than investing in a specialist collection. Here is my reasoning. Most of us, as we pass through our lives acquire a house and then gradually the contents, much of these the essentials of modern living such as furniture, kitchenalia, the accoutrements of dining or the tools of gardening and the decorative touches which make a house into a home. To add some statistics to the story, in 2008 the average annual buildings insurance in the UK was just over £200 and the average contents insurance £151. Most of us take out between £50,000 and £80,000 worth of contents insurance a year, to replace old with new in the event of a catastrophe such as a fire or flood. If we were to sell the contents of our homes most people would only raise the smallest fraction of the average of £65,000. The reason is obvious. Most people have 'invested' in new goods. Even when carrying out valuations of worthwhile collections I am disappointed that in many cases no thought has been given to the investment potential that can be added into building a home, indeed sometimes the collection is worth far more than the rest of the contents put together even though more money would have been spent in building the home than building the collection. The problem with buying new is that when goods are removed from the store they are worth a fraction of their cost. It doesn't matter whether it is furniture or a dinner service or cutlery or ornaments or pictures. Furniture is the worst because the 'investment' is considerable and the potential loss all the greater. What I am suggesting is that buying new is rarely the most prudent use of the family budget. Not only is new furniture often poor value for money but a lot of the cheaper stock is made of poor materials, as one auctioneer called it the '.com wonder stock' which you will have to replace every few years. I recommend an alternative. In the market place today are three or four hundred years of secondhand goods across every category of collecting or household use. There are styles to suit every personality and every home and remember that the housing stock embraces a similar period. Much is sold at a fraction of the mark up of high street stores and is good value for money if you buy from the right sources. I am not advising you turn your home into a museum but I am suggesting not only the economy in buying secondhand or antique but also the possibility of investment potential, certainly in the longer term. In a recent edition of *Antiques Info* I published the *ACC Antique Furniture Index* for 2007. The Index began in 1968 when it stood at 100. At the end of 2007 it stood at 2982. In other words antique furniture has in thirty years increased thirty fold in value, equivalent to the increase in value of the stock market in the same period. Buying new makes no economic sense whatsoever. Nor does buying the whole range of new reproductions of every commodity that are displayed and advertised in magazines that usually have the word 'Period' in their title. There is nothing period whatsoever about these goods and they suffer the same crash in value once removed from the store. Take jewellery. The current average high street retail mark up is 225%. Buying a diamond ring with say half a carat of stones could typically cost you £799. Buy at auction and you will pay about £300-400. Should you be buying new pictures for the wall which one day may end up in a charity shop? In the secondhand market you could be buying original art or Lowry prints, the choice is so much greater. I despair at the limited edition figurines around which one day can only end up with the same fate. I worry when yet another new cutlery service is bought when the secondhand market is overflowing with quality sets from the classic early twentieth century at a fraction of the price and which will hold their value and could prove an investment over time.

9

Chapter II

Investing in Information and Knowledge

In the first chapter I was deliberately controversial in setting out a quite definitive philosophy for collecting. Where angels fear to tread? I openly criticised what I considered the absurd notion, peddled continuously by certain media experts, that collecting was, and shouldn't be considered anything other than a pleasure and that any realised investment was a bonus. Rather I placed the emphasis on the importance of always ensuring that collectors make prudent, sensible and shrewd purchases with investment firmly in mind. In short, I leaned considerably to one side of the 'serendipity versus investment' debate! Furthermore I argued that collectors shouldn't waste money buying from the lower end of the market and should slap their own wrists long before they end up with a house full of affectionate junk that they cannot move on except to a charity shop. This argument was summarised as the 'commonplace versus the worthwhile' debate. More importantly I argued for the notion of the whole home as an investment area, for generalising as well as specialising and I used statistics to back up my arguments in what I summarised as the 'old versus new' debate. Implicit in these arguments was a thread, a theme intended to underpin the whole philosophy. Prudent and shrewd investing, or successful collecting and dealing can only be achieved through study. Knowledge and information are the keys that will open a lot of doors.

Investing in Information and Knowledge

Some twenty five years ago I remember visiting an antiques shop somewhere in England and an incident occurred which will serve well to illustrate the above point. Many similar incidents have occurred since but this one has stuck very firmly in my mind. I was studying a quite extensive range of pottery and porcelain on offer in the antiques shop and noticed that a small decorative teapot, clearly of twentieth century origin and made of continental hardpaste porcelain, had been ascribed on the label to J Heath, (Joshua Heath, Hanley, Staffordshire) and dated as c1800. I turned over the teapot and found that it was impressed 'JH'. Now certainly Joshua Heath was working in Hanley in that period but he only manufactured pottery, not porcelain and certainly not a continental hardpaste. Now we can excuse the fact that if this had been made by Joshua Heath, the old form IH would have been used in this period. And I don't even wish to consider that this was a very knowledgeable dealer pulling a fast one. Rather it was my opinion at the time that the dealer had simply looked up the mark in *The Encyclopaedia of British Pottery and Porcelain*, by Geoffrey A. Godden, when, if he had identified the type as a continental paste he should have been searching in Ludwig Danckert's *Directory of European Porcelain*, both incidentally essential books for the ceramics collector. All of the signs were there to see for anybody who had studied even just the basics of the subject. The shape was wrong, the material was wrong, the decoration was twentieth century. Similarly and more recently in an entirely different part of the country I was able to buy an English soft paste Chelsea-Derby classical figure, c1770, marked up as twentieth century, that is 1960s, and priced at only £12! Worse still, they said I could have it for £8. These anecdotes make the point. Investing in information and knowledge, and marrying study to the right kinds of academic experiences are the keys to successful collecting and dealing. Below I have made suggestions as to how collectors can gain the right kinds of experiences.

Collectors' Clubs

All of these ingredients come together in collectors' clubs. I learned my ceramics in the *Canterbury Ceramics Circle*. The monthly meetings brought together a dozen to a score of people whose combined experience and knowledge represented hundreds of years of study and dedication to their hobby. At most meetings new finds were passed around and exposed to the opinions, judgements and analyses of an august group of dedicated collectors. Such scrutiny provided the most intense and pleasurable learning experience. In addition there were lectures by visiting experts, well known figures in their field and field trips to visit collections as well as social occasions such as Christmas dinners. I have seen collectors, after only a very few years of exposure to such an experience become successful dealers in their own right, able to handle with confidence and identify, almost every ceramic type from the last 300 years! At this level, marks only assist in the analysis, they are not the basis of it, as was the case with our dealer with the teapot!

You can find out about your local collectors' clubs through the library services or go on-line. To check this approach I typed 'huddersfield collectors club' into Google. This led me to the community local organisations run by Kirklees Council and gave me a further information email address of kinfo@kirklees.gov.uk. On the same page was the *Collectors' Club of Huddersfield*. According to the on-line information this is one of the UKs premier clubs. They run events, have displays of antiques and collectibles and guest speakers. They boast a local membership and world-wide postal members. They run a quarterly magazine called *The Bulletin*. New members and guests are welcome. They also provide free advice on valuations and disposal of collections. They run a small auction after each meeting and there is also swapping as well as socialising. Junior members are also welcome. There is a phone number and an address and a link to **www.multimap.com**. I have clicked on this link and viewed a street map for HD1 5BZ with the location of the *Collectors' Club of Huddersfield* marked. I can zoom out to view the wider area and there is even a further link to multimap where you can key in your own address details and print off directions. Of course if you have 'sat nav' fitted to your car you can key in the postcode and it will talk you in. When you leave just key in 'home' and the 'sat nav' will talk you back again. Apart from local clubs there are also national and international clubs and societies covering every aspect of the antiques and collecting industry. I can go to our own website at **www.antiques-info.co.uk** where our own Gold Services members can log into our *Clubs, Associations and Societies Database* and search out any contact details they require. For example if a subscriber types 'poole' into the search facility our database will find the *Poole Pottery Collectors' Club*. For those subscribers to our magazine who are not on line we deal with any information requests by post or telephone.

Antiques Courses

Another area which marries study to hands-on experiences and contact with experts is to sign up to an academic course. Again you can find out about courses through your local library services. Every need is catered for. There are courses at every level and of every duration. You can sign up to anything from a local night class introducing you to collecting or take a masters degree. You can attend degree courses at *Southampton Institute* or study at home with tutorial support. The variety of opportunity is endless. If you are on-line just key 'antiques courses' into a search engine and you will be almost overwhelmed by the choice. The Web is an extensive and perhaps unlimited source of information but also a huge buying and selling arena. We will be returning to this in greater depth in **Chapter III** when I turn, for the first time to discussing the market. Meanwhile, having touched on books earlier in this discussion let me now examine in much greater depth a media which dominates all others as a reliable source of information and study. It has done so since the beginning of recorded history and still remains so today.

The Importance of Books

The importance of the written word to mankind cannot be overstated and the rapid advances made in digital technology and word processing has not altered this one little bit. Despite the computer age, books continue to be published as never before. I receive at least half a dozen new books to review every week, and these are only a part of the almost burgeoning output. Our office library now contains about 2,000 books on collecting despite regular clear outs, and believe me there are plenty of books that would have been better never written. However on a daily basis I still spend longer studying books than I do surfing the web, still firmly believing more in the veracity of the printed word than its digital equivalent, and certainly where it involves analysis rather than straightforward information. The world of books remains alive and well, with some qualifications!

Whereas the functional parameters of a book require that it is not too large or too small or too light or too heavy for storage purposes, along with looking good of course, often these seem to be the main considerations, along with making money for the publisher of course! Our industry unfortunately has more than its fair share of such books. They continue to appear in increasing numbers. Such books are usually frivolous. They might for example be telling you about the antiques of the future and advising on where you should be spending your money. They may claim to be letting you into their secrets about collecting but of course this is the last thing they would do if they actually had any, which of course they have not. They are at best very light and perhaps entertaining if your heart is still filled with the wonder of childhood, but reading such books can only be a pastime and as you will have now gathered, I consider collecting a much more important occupation, almost as serious perhaps as was Bill Shankley's assessment of the importance of football, more than just a life and death matter!

As with antiques and collectables, so it is the same with books. Some are worthwhile and most are irrelevant. Yet, despite my cynicism, at the outset of the main paragraphs of this study I must clearly state that collecting books about collecting is probably more important than collecting itself. Serious books in my judgement fall into several categories and it is important to make some early distinctions. For practical purposes and for the purposes of discussion these fall neatly into say, five types. My first type may be termed the typical library type. These books sweep across the whole world of antiques, often supporting the text with imagery from museum collections. Their usefulness is strictly limited to a simplified introduction to the subject. I call these 'library types' because this is the best place for them. Once browsed and cherry-picked for the categories of antiques that interest you they are rarely opened ever again. To make the point even further, try selling such books to a secondhand book dealer and you will see what I mean. Even charity shops turn them down. They can't even sell the ones they've got.

My second type of book is still generalised but at least it is also themed and as such is more desirable. As examples I might suggest, say a book on Gothic art, or the Art Nouveau movement or on world glass. I have such books in my collection but again they are far too generalised to be of much practical use. Once browsed they are rarely if ever referred to again. To once again make the point, try selling to a secondhand book dealer. He or she will be more interested but a pound or two will be the most they will offer, even in unused condition with a £30 to £50 RRP price tag. In fact the secondhand book dealer is the real yardstick. After all they are the experts when it comes to book values.

Of course what they are really seeking, and so should we all, are what I will call my third type of book, known in the academic world as the monograph. These works represent a treatise on a single object or subject or more commonly in the world of collecting a class of objects or a single subject. Not all books of course fit neatly into my arbitrary types but like any attempted classification they serve a purpose. And these are the books that hold their values even when secondhand and some, when they become scarce even increase in value, like antiques themselves. In art such a book may be a specialised work on sea painters or more specifically a study of a particular artist such as Herbert Draper or Charles Brooking. In ceramics such books may cover a particular output such as Spode or a type such as parian or creamware, fairings or Staffordshire or *Pot-Lids* or *Cats in English Porcelain*. But whether a study of a single output, such as Rockingham or Whitefriars, or a study of Georgian drinking glasses or treen or Christopher Dresser, these are the types of book that are important to the dealer and the book dealer as well as the collector. Never stint on books and in particular those that are considered the bibles in their field. I cannot think of a single monograph in my collection that has not repaid itself over and over again.

My fourth type are price guides and sometimes these are also incorporated into monographs such as *Pot-Lids* by K. V. Mortimer, which is also an excellent reference work. Other price guides, which are also good reference works, have assumed almost biblical importance in their field such as the **Coin Year Book** and the **Medal Yearbook** produced by Token Publishing or the annual **Picture Postcard Values** by Phil and Dave Smith or **Cigarette Card Values** by Murray. One of the better known series of specialist price guides are the **Charlton Standard Catalogues** which deal with a range of twentieth century ceramics such as Doulton and Beswick. They are of vital importance to many thousands of collectors because they deal in the particular in the finest of detail. As reference works they are superb but as price guides it is my judgement that they are unreliable, tending towards trying to lead the market rather than follow. In our own way we produce price guides on specific areas of the market such as ceramics furniture, silver and jewellery and glass. Each of our price guides contains at least 3,000 images, descriptions and prices from actual sales but these books are straightforward guides to the market and an analysis of the market. They are not monographs in the broader sense. In general the more general the price guide the less useful it becomes. History itself can never be about the generality of the past, if so it is in danger of becoming legend. Only in the particular might we find the truth. It is a sad fact that price guides have had a lot of bad press in recent years but there are a lot of good ones around and the general situation is improving. Miller's tell us that they are basing prices on actual sales and I am aware that they are doing their very best to ensure that their prices reflect the market.

My final type are the marks books. I mentioned earlier, two that are the bibles in their field. There are also a range of excellent marks books in other fields. A book on silver marks is essential and Foulsham produce an excellent book on silver plate marks as well as an extremely useful Dealer Guide to *Victorian Painters' Monograms*. I have personally been able to identify artists from this work and once a name can be attached to a painting it usually adds to its value. An excellent marks book which has recently been published in its second edition is *British Studio Potters' Marks* by Eric Yates-Owen and Robert Fournier. Collecting the right kinds of books are the best investments you can ever make. Readers can purchase any book currently in print by ordering through their local bookshop. Or on-line a useful website for the purchase of new and secondhand books is **bookfinder.com**.

The Cons and the Pros of Television

Finally the most controversial area of all. Several million of us seem to enjoy watching television programmes on collecting and why not? *Going for a Song* was the first and the *Antiques Roadshow* has enjoyed a hugely successful run. The format is excellent, worthwhile and serious enough to be educational. Other programmes are more controversial and produce mixed reactions. Typically they depend on an angle or a game show format that leans heavily towards entertainment. The reality of the market, which acts as a backdrop to the enactments, is frequently skewed or even seriously compromised. *Bargain Hunt* has introduced an educational cameo into its format but it is brief. In 2007 the industry, not the BBC I might add, came under fire for misleading the public in the matter of the competition phone-in row which was of course a serious matter. I disagree with these game show formats because they tend to make monkeys out of us all. When the BBC had its licence renewed a few years ago it promised a more serious and educational approach but this hasn't happened. Indeed much of the content of even BBC news programmes is in itself becoming trivial. Many pundits within the antiques and collecting industry deplore the cameras. Many dealers and events organisers feel the same way and refuse them access. I have been told that they don't pay a penny but I am willing to be corrected if this is not the case! Others however welcome them with open arms: the publicity they bring can be a bonus. One thing is certain they show little respect for the industry at large and the dealer in particular. I suppose the best thing is to take a more equitable approach and accept that it is the nature of television and the film industry in general to entertain rather than to tell it straight. After all they have been pulling the wool over our eyes since the earliest days of the silent movies. Little has changed. Sit back therefore and be entertained and if you get too serious about what is happening before your very eyes, then make sure you keep the salt handy and take a pinch every so often.

Chapter III

An Introduction to the Antiques & Collecting Market

Before dealing in the four main areas of the market, that is the fairs scene, the auctions industry, the retail sector and the internet, and the way the market in all of its various facets works, I would like to spend some time examining the market in general. In other words before we get lost in the trees, let us step back and look at the wood, or to put it another way take a more philosophical approach about the industry at large. This should enable us to avoid forming any pre-conceived opinions or making unsound judgements about how the industry works. It should prevent us holding or forming any prejudices or biases against any particular aspects of the market and of course it should also ensure that we avoid viewing the industry through rose coloured spectacles. In other words we will see the industry much more clearly if we adopt, at the outset, an equitable approach to its charms as well as its to its more, and sometimes less obvious failings.

The sheer diversity of the market, and now the internet, assures our fascination and the fascination of millions with its continuously unfolding story. Basically it is all about people in time and the artefacts they have created. It is about human intelligence and human endeavour. It is about the human family tree and our place in history. It is about the past, the present and the future in respect of how we make our personal marks. It is about our ancestry, about our nostalgia, about our personal needs and our personal ambitions. It is about serendipity and it is about making money in our time or investing in our future and the future of our children.

Onto this stage tread royalty, the nobility and the nouveau riche, investing their millions in perhaps more millions. Onto this stage tread crooks as well as connoisseurs: academics, historians, librarians, curators and curates, doctors and down-and-outs, professionals and amateurs, experts and pundits, television and the press, the unwary and the wary, the sly and the naive, exploiters and the exploited, parsons and punters seeking their own particular pot of gold, rainbow's end or the winning lottery ticket. Whether the setting is the glitz of a royal gala evening at the Grosvenor or yet another boring boot fair in Basildon the motivation is the same, the glister of gold in whatever form it takes or the pleasure of the human experience. For here can be found a Monet for millions, exquisite antiques and art of unsurpassed rarity, undiscovered treasures of incalculable value, the worthwhile and the mundane, the junk and the dross and the debris of societies past and present. And in some areas of the market, new masquerading as old, the invidious creations of man's duplicity: and even worse, fakes, the insidious craft of his treachery.

It is a well known fact that there are many who distrust the antiques market. Such a prejudice extends to the absurd generalisation that dealers cannot be trusted and that the industry at large is seedy and shady. Even the notion of secondhand is anathema to many, so they fill their homes with notional 'period' replicas or reproductions of every household commodity, paying as much or more than they would for the real thing. Even now, as the twenty-first century progresses and the notion of 'vintage' begins to extend well beyond its earlier restriction to women's fashions, the suspicious and the smug are turning to Ikea and other warehouses to buy reproductions of twentieth century 'retro', at prices in excess of the originals. I am sure there is far more repro in the new than in the secondhand market. Ridiculous when there are now even fairs specialising in the real retro! Where on earth did we go wrong? The answer I am sure is complex, but I am also sure that certain parts of the industry could make a start by rooting out all of those invidious and the more insidious elements of so called 'antiques and collectibles' that are now appearing in many uncontrolled environments. I will be discussing this in the next chapters when I take a closer look at the different areas of the market. In the meantime let me tackle the prejudices.

The fallacy of the shady market
The main defence is that in the main those that think ill of our industry couldn't be further from the truth, or to put it bluntly they are wrong! Many dealers, in fact the great majority are scrupulous in their activities and as honest as the day is long. Most are small businesses making an honest living and working to tight margins. They are motivated far more by job satisfaction than profit. Ignore the hyperbole of television game shows where competitors are offered huge discounts at fairs and in antiques centres. This is an unfair manipulation of the market in the interests of entertainment. It is a discredit to the antiques trade and an insult to us all, and it is about time it stopped, particularly in the BBC, where one should expect licence payers' money to be put to a more credible and a more creditable use.

Most readers will agree that it is the macro companies and industries where the commercial imperatives drive greater and greater profits. If we want to highlight a dearth of scruples or dodgy business ethics then let us turn to some of the major players in the commercial scene where profits are measured in billions and scruples by the grain! This is the real world where fat profits feed fast cars and fast life styles, not the antiques and collecting industry. Leading the way, and they would know all about it, wouldn't they, is the financial services sector, the most complained about of all. Can you be certain that you have been given the best advice about your pension or that your bank or insurance company is playing fair? Despite the continuing bad press they remain as resilient as ever and impervious to censure or to shame. And what about the utilities, private companies now who, despite the censures of watchdogs and punitive fines ride higher and higher on unjustified profits and unbelievedly, the hot air of public hostility. And can you really feel sure that you are getting the best price when you are travelling by train or would you feel more certain of success if you tackled the rubik cube? Does your company pay out bonuses when it fails to achieve its targets? And are you happy that top managers across the civil services are paid bonuses often in excess of the annual salaries of lower paid workers? And even the rubik cube may be easier solved than trying to work out some of the special offer conundrums in your local hypermarket, or whether to use your mobile phone abroad.

Of course there are also problems in our industry, and I will be airing them later. But these are small compared to the loaded guns of the commercial giants that are pointing at our heads whilst the managers hide behind the camouflage of the call centres. The real face of the shady deal is more often than not dressed in city clothes, lives in the very best part of town and with certainty never drives a secondhand car, like most dealers. Hyperbole of course, with perhaps a dash of prejudice thrown in, but I have my tongue firmly in my cheek. Now I will be taking a closer look at the antiques and collecting market, still at its macro level, in respect of its attractions and its investment potential balanced against its more, and sometimes less obvious failings.

The fallacy of the bargain
Bargains can be bad as well as good and sometimes even very experienced collectors and dealers can make mistakes. This said the notion of the good bargain should never be the focus for beginners. Once you have gained your experience and knowledge in your chosen field or fields of expertise then the occasional windfall will come along, but by their nature these are going to be few and far between. In general the aims should be to make purchases that are worthwhile and not frivolous, that you will enjoy, and then also to consider if you wish, their long term investment potential in the light of your knowledge of the market.

The nature of the market
It is the nature of all universal markets that they may experience long term stability and even short term volatility. I like to look on long term stability as being associated with the longer term prevailing fashions and customs. Alternatively there are also the more long term and short term trends in the market which of course will end up at some point with a certain amount of volatility. If this follows a long term trend then the volatility may represent no more than a market reappraisal or adjustment due to certain current universal factors such as an economic slump and is unlikely to affect the longer term investments. However short term trends and their associated volatility may well result in burnt fingers. I will provide examples of both. The universal factors in the market are those that I consider will affect the whole market and are outside of the control of any single collector.

Long term stability
Forty years ago the *Antique Collectors' Club* produced their Furniture Price Index and this has been an annual event ever since.The Index tracks prices and compares them with the stock market and the housing market and the retail price index, or in other words inflation. For thirty six years good antique furniture has proved to be a better investment than either the stock market or houses and has also kept well above the annual inflation figures until prices began to fall in about 2004/5. The doom mongers were soon forecasting a slump but in fact it was no more than a reappraisal in difficult trading conditions and the furniture market has now made a small recovery and is even better placed than ever to offer investment potential. It currently stands at about 3000 or thirty times its 1969 value. One thing is certain and beyond dispute. Antique furniture has proved to be a very sound investment over time whereas buying new would have proved no investment whatsoever. Incidentally, when furniture prices stuttered and went into reverse for a few years certain pundits were quick to point up the continuing rises in the stock market and the housing market, but their declines have been even more severe than antique furniture and as one would expect they are more volatile. Furniture is one of the biggest expenses that home owners face in their home building years and the antiques and secondhand market provides the greatest variety, the better average quality and the better value for money when

compared to the new equivalent. And in addition our recent history suggests that it is also one of the best investment areas. I had a conversation recently with an acquaintance who was explaining to me that he considered that he had covered all areas in terms of investing for his family's future. He had substantial cash savings in various accounts earning the best interests available. He had ISA's and played the stock market where he was enjoying some modest success, although I doubt if that is continuing. He was ploughing money back into his business enterprises and was now taking a look at gilts and bonds, which he said would complete his investment portfolio. I think he is missing out because he seemed completely unaware of the investment potential of art and antiques.

Another good long term investment and certainly in the last ten years has been precious metals and good jewellery. The ten-year line graphs for silver, gold and platinum show a steady upward trend although most gains have been in the last five years. Now in 2010 prices are buoyant and the market has picked up at all levels whereas it has been the top end of the market in most other categories that have benefited in recent years whilst the middle and lower markets have fallen away, mainly because prices for many collectibles had become inflated and were beyond the means of the average collector. Whereas the high current prices of precious metals may have something to do with a weak dollar and China buying into the commodities it is interesting to look at how diamonds, and in our case diamond jewellery are fairing. Here again is a category which has proved over the long term to be a good investment. Prices are flying and this is an area where you can invest in modern jewellery or the classic period of the late nineteenth and early twentieth centuries. I find it interesting that in times when science has provided diamonds that are manufactured and not mined, this has not dented the value of the real thing one little bit. In fact the opposite is the case as the well-heeled and the well-manicured continue to demand the best. It is the same with pearls. Despite the fact that the Chinese in the 1990s developed the ability to produce perfect salt water pearls cultured in freshwater mussels the demand for original saltwater sets is undiminished. We don't have to dwell only on the top end of the market however. If you want to invest in jewellery at all levels of the market you are far better off in the secondhand market where prices are traditionally only about 40% of what you will pay on the high street. About the worst thing you can do is buy the junk jewellery from the latest digital channels on television. **Trading Standards** could well do with looking in on some of these programmes. Recently I listened to one presenter describing an item as solid nine carat gold!

The foregoing represent two categories of antiques worth looking at in the sense that both traditional antique furniture and jewellery are functional, worthwhile collecting areas, as well as offering investment potential. They can be identified in 2010 as potentially offering long term stability because they have in the past. It would also be possible to identify other traditional collecting areas that have stood the test of time or seek and collect the worthwhile in almost any category of collecting. It is also possible however to collect or invest or spend your money in areas that pose far more of a risk. Two examples should suffice.

Short term volatility

Throughout the last two thirds of the twentieth century and on-going into the twenty-first century many of the well known ceramics outputs have been turning out figurines by the millions which they sell of course to those who only buy new goods, and the carrot is usually yet another figure in the series or the latest limited edition. They even re-issue earlier issues, often from years earlier and inevitably the market has suffered a setback. It has become now a case of death from a thousand figurines, only in reality there are probably several billion out there. The related price guides don't help with their over-optimistic listings. What a great pity. Even the Royal Worcester Freda Doughty figurines have become devalued as have many Royal Doulton examples and there seems to be no end to the manufactures. This is currently a very volatile area of collecting and not one that I would be investing in although I am certain that it is still possible to make worthwhile purchases on a selective basis. But how can you know that the factories will not re-issue the rarer models? Let us take a further example, a very safe and certain collecting area, that of Moorcroft pottery. This output is of course still in production and I have seen recently that a large Moorcroft vase, *After the Storm,* made for the 1997 Centenary in a limited edition of 200, fetched £1,587 at auction. Now I personally wouldn't pay that much money for a vase knowing that there are another 199 out there, but I could be wrong, such is the demand for pieces of quality. The point really is that whilst early Moorcroft of quality, at the very top end of the market has been an excellent investment there must of necessity be a far greater degree of speculation in buying modern Moorcroft.

Of course the twentieth century in general has seen a lot of interest in recent years spurred on by much media hyperbole. The notion of 'what's hot' has been frequently on the lips of so called television experts and as a result many fingers have been burnt as prices have collapsed. It is quite ridiculous anyway to think of buying things when they are already at a premium and are likely to have only one direction in which they are likely to go. Many collectors have been foolishly paying crazy money in the last few years for twentieth century pottery and porcelain, simply because it has been in the news. I have been amazed to see, and I am still seeing, prices being asked around the country for common or garden teawares that would be more apt if they were applied to First Period Worcester! In an earlier part of this story I referred to the silly books being published by so called television personalities on the back of their 'fame' where they recommend their 'antiques of the future.' Always these recommendations are an almost complete travesty of what collectors should really be buying. Of course the golden rule for investing in antiques is to firstly check out the form of the items which interest you and then to be familiar enough with the market to know that the prices that are being asked are reasonable or even keen. Then the next golden rule is to buy the very best you can afford and take at least a medium to long term view. After all you will be living with and of course enjoying your investments for a very long time. The good thing about art and antiques is that they become part of your persona and part of your home and they tend to hang around much better than the more easily spent cash savings. Even if they only match inflation in the longer term it means that you still have your investment, or you might call it your savings, and that it hasn't disap-peared over several new cars or exotic holidays or for that matter meals out.

My second example of a dodgy investment area is the modern art market. With so much money swimming around the city, 2008 saw a surge in sales and a surge in prices for twentieth century art and the works of living artists. This was related to the flattening of prices in the traditional investment areas, such as nineteenth century landscapes, so the big money turned towards the twentieth century. There was nothing wrong with this but the intense activity in this area of the market at the top end was feeding down to the ordinary punters with a few hundred to spare each month and they were buying art in all forms, some of which they had no chance of ever selling let alone of getting any return on their money. Some were buying the most absurd 'Tate Modern' type stuff. To give an example, I know an acquaintance who bought a modern oil which had actually been painted on a fridge door, and now he can't get rid of it so it has ended up in his loft. Well, he can hardly hang it on a wall as I am certain his wife would give him the cold shoulder! Yet twentieth century art is an excellent investment area providing you have the expertise and the market knowledge to seize the opportunities, which appear more often than you might think. This is why specialising is so important. It ensures that you can spend with confidence.

The micro market and a further fallacy in the collecting industry
It is time now to look at those factors in the market place that operate at the micro level as opposed to the macro level in that they are not universal factors and are therefore within the control of the buyer or the collector. One of the most important considerations in my judgement is the fallacy of a wholesale/retail dichotomy within the industry in respect of prices. A leading and indispensable price guide series, the *Charlton Press* clearly state in their introductory pages that auctions are wholesale and that they base their price lists on retail. They add that to equate both prices they need to adjust auctions results upwards by a minimum of 100%. I have shown time and again in the pages of *Antiques Info* by using actual sales results from the auctions industry and then comparing them with their price guide listings that, at all levels of the market this arithmetic simply does not work. Time and time again their listings are up to 200 and sometimes 300% more than comparable auctions results, whilst less frequently there can be even a degree of parity, which is not supposed to be the case either. Sometimes the listings work but it is a complete lottery and this is certainly not a basis on which to suggest values. At the top end of the market, and when the rarer and more desirable figures appear for sale at auction they frequently fetch more and sometimes much more than the book prices! Their policy also assumes that it is only the trade who buy at auction, who then sell at retail with about a 100% mark up. Chance would be a fine thing! In fact the auctions industry is not a closed shop like the Trade warehouse in the new goods sector. The salerooms are open to all, dealers and collectors alike. Prices on the day are influenced by a whole range of factors and whilst there is a predictability relating to prices which are published as estimates in respect of many lots, because the market is very knowledgeable about values, there can never be any foregone conclusions and therefore auctions results are not a basis on which to produce price guides based on a simplistic formula that reduces the auctions' participation to a wholesale role. There is no dichotomy and the beginner should be prepared to study the whole market and buy in all areas of the market, depending on their specialism. At times though, in their collecting career, it is possible that they might regret not buying from a specialist dealer who will be aware of all the very latest pitfalls in the wider market. After all his or her business depends on it.

Marketing and the market
The prospective buyer should also be aware of the implications of marketing on the saleability of antiques and collectibles. This may be sales talk or suggestive descriptions or perhaps the disarming persuasion of canapés and champagne. Whatever, it is rarely the

problem that it has become in the new goods or services sector. Two examples from the world of finance will suffice. A few years ago I had a few thousand pounds to invest so checked out all of the rates on our high street then settled for an Alliance & Leicester account which, in large bold type on the advertising leaflet, offered a further 0.5% interest, over and above the standard interest on the account, at the end of the first year, and so on. When I opened the account I checked with the cashier that this was indeed the case. About nine months later I received a letter from the Alliance & Leicester advising me that they were closing down that particular type of account and that I needed to transfer my money to their standard account which of course didn't pay the extra 0.5% after a year. I complained to the manager but he pointed to the small print on the back of the leaflet. Sure enough one of the conditions allowed the Alliance & Leicester to close the account at any time. Now I doubt in law that a financial institution is permitted to offer contending conditions on the same account, but the manager was adamant that he had no case to answer. He was quite put out when I closed the account for good and with immediate effect. Another example of financial jiggery-pokery was on offer in 2008 by my current bank, HSBC. Their Bank Account Plus was being widely advertised in June 2008 under the banner headline of 8% AER and of course this is only 7.72% gross and for tax payers about 6.176% net. Now to the small print. This rate only applies to the first £1,000 which works out at about £61.76 interest in a year. The rate falls to a very poor 2.47% gross or about 1.976% net up to £2,500 and then to an absurd 0.1% gross or or about 0.08% net above that! Worse still there was a monthly fee to pay of £12.95 and a minimum one year contract so the first year fees will cost £155.40 and based on the first £1,000 produce a net annual loss of £93.64, which of course can only, in practice, be very marginally offset by balances over a £1,000, and made worse by an average annual balance under a £1,000. Another aspect of this type of HSBC account is that the headline figure included a bonus element and that you lost this bonus element of the total interest paid during the whole of the month in which you make any withdrawals. There are additional benefits, the best of which is free worldwide family travel insurance which could put you back in the black, but there are restrictions, the most invidious being an age limit of seventy, which is highly questionable ethically and may flout European legislation. I tried this account and lost money on it.

Consumer protection
Fortunately we do not have to put up with these types of dubious practices when collecting, and if we ever feel that we are being short-changed in any way, most times we can do something about it, or go elsewhere. It is also important to realise that in the antiques and collecting industry that you can shop at many different levels and that there are many fairs and auctions and retail outlets that provide a high degree of consumer protection through their trade institutions. Collectors should give some thought to the degree of protection available in antiques centres. As far as I know the onus falls on the individual dealer, so read on to find out how you should guard against the possibility of mis-selling. And whilst buying at auction can be very daunting for the beginner, most fine art auctions, being often established local businesses that might go back even a century or more, can offer you all the help and advice you need to make sound purchases. If auctions are too daunting, in the learning years, there are many excellent dealers in the market place who operate to a code of conduct and provide exceptional levels of service. I will be discussing the various

elements of the market in much further detail in the next several chapters. In the meantime it is worth discussing some of the pitfalls that may be encountered in the general market place and what steps the collector can take to minimise the risks of making spurious purchases.

The more obvious pitfalls

Nothing can replace knowledge and experience and in time those who specialise and study their subject will be able to make sound judgements in almost every kind of market situation. Meanwhile it is important that the collector learns to think firstly outside of the actual buying situation and more about the level of consumer protection that exists in any particular buying environment. Your legal rights will count for nothing if you bought something from an antiques and collectors fair a 150 miles away, without a receipt and without knowing anything about the dealer who sold you the goods. This kind of buying is going on all of the time and whilst these kinds of situations are not always going to suit the faint hearted or the inexperienced or the unwary, don't get paranoid about being conned. You will fare much better, most of the time than you will in the new goods sector even if you take no precautions whatsoever! Specialist collectors/dealers often profit from these situations by buying from dealers with less specialist knowledge than themselves.

The next potential pitfall in the buying experience is labelling. I have already provided examples of labelling from the wider market and the general level of ethical standards within the commercial world at large leaves much to be desired. For example last week a certain bottle of wine in a supermarket was £3.99. This week it is still £3.99 but is being sold as a special offer with a £1 off. The labelling pronounces 'Was £4.99.' Or another I have remembered were packs of onions on a Sainsbury shelf advertised as 'Save a £1 per kilogram,' but the actual packs were only three quarters of a kilogram, so the saving was only 75 pence. The manager insisted that the labelling was ethical and refused to accept my argument that it was misleading. And do you know, I actually believe that he believed that he was right because this kind of marketing has become instinctive and fair game in the world of commerce. Undaunted I asked him to seek the opinions of the next ten shoppers who passed by in respect of how much was actually being saved, but he declined. This is not the usual level of standards in our industry and most labelling is as honest as the day is long.Where there are problems in labelling these are mainly down to the dealers lack of knowledge or a straightforward error. Many dealers can carry a range of goods and they simply don't have the expertise to be absolutely accurate in their labelling 100% of the time. As I have stated already this can often be a benefit as much as it can be a problem, especially if you are the expert. This said the beginner must also be prepared for labelling which may contain deliberately misleading content or as often as not omissions related to the description or the age or the condition. I also find that it also wise to be suspicious when the labelling is no more than a price, or the item is not labelled at all. I recently examined a Georgian rummer and two small landscape oils that had been bought at different times from an antiques centre by a relative of mine. The buyer had an invoice for the glass, which stated it was Georgian, and as it was almost new he was subsequently able to get a refund. I cannot say that the error was deliberate or a genuine mistake on the part of the dealer. Such glasses are difficult for the general dealer and I will accept that it was an honest mistake. Alternatively the two pictures were landscapes in the style of the early twentieth century, as were the frames, and one carried an applied paper label which looked just as old as the painting because it was a copy of an original label. The buyer had paid only decorative prices for the paintings, about £65 for the two, but genuinely believed them to be about a 100 years old. Now I will accept that you really cannot buy genuine paintings like this for £65, and of course these also turned out to be brand new. The buyer was very unhappy at being 'deceived,' but in this case hadn't bothered to ask for an invoice. In fact I judge the painting with the label to be a fake if it had been mis-sold. Unfortunately the buyer didn't ask the right questions and the dealer didn't enlighten him. If the buyer had asked the appropriate questions in the first place, then I am certain that the dealer would have been truthful, therefore probably losing the sale. Now we have a very unhappy buyer and the centre has lost a good customer. It is exactly these kinds of situations that give the trade a bad name. Here there was absolutely no consumer protection whatsoever and the centre was carrying potentially fake stock and displaying it in circumstances where the unwary may be misled and the inexperienced even deceived. Surely when you visit an antiques centre you should expect to find old and not new goods. And if there are new goods on display then surely they should be labelled as such. There is of course fault with the buyer. Firstly it is no shame if you are considering buying in an area outside of your experience to ask as many questions as you feel you need in order to make a buying decision. Secondly you should always ask for an invoice and this invoice should contain, not only a full description of the purchase, but also the approximate age or age range. The invoice should also contain details of the condition of the purchase including any damage, renovation or restoration. These three elements should be present, where appropriate on all invoices and if the dealer is unwilling to include such details on, what amounts to your legal proof of purchase, then walk away. I also advise keeping a record of all purchases in a stock book. This can be a godsend years later when you no longer remember the details or even how much you paid at the time.

Reproductions and fakes
Finally a further word on reproductions and fakes. Reproductions have been around for a long time and in themselves are harmless provided they are sold as such. The new goods sector sells them all of the time. Many reproductions are themselves now antiques in their own right. There is even a market for new reproductions. Yet there can be no doubt that the invasion of reproductions into many areas of the market is detrimental to the market and has dented consumer confidence and turned prospective collectors away. Their invidious presence, often in circumstances which can cause irritation, even annoyance and certainly suspicion are a blight on the industry at large and it is a sad fact that certain areas of the market do not practice more control. And of course a reproduction can become a fake when it is mis-sold. In the example of the oil paintings I have no doubt that these were not mis-sold but the circumstances are worrying enough to suggest that they would have been better marked up as new in the first place. Far worse is the insidious and intentional fake and these are around in many categories of antiques and collectibles. Many are now so realistic that it takes an expert to spot them. Sometimes when a lot of money is at stake it is wise to buy from a specialist dealer or auction. Such vetting at least ensures the authenticity of your purchase and could save you money in the long run.

Chapter IV

The Fairs Market

In the last chapter I made a comprehensive study of the market in general. I also looked at the nature of the antiques and collecting market and at certain widely held fallacies. I examined the long term stability and the short term volatility of the market. I introduced and touched on the notion of the macro-market, over which as individual collectors or dealers, we have no control, and the micro market, where our expertise and our knowledge and our own actions will either turn us into very competent collectors or dealers, or else expose us to the pitfalls that on occasions are waiting to mislead the unwary or even deceive those who may have little experience of collecting. The more obvious pitfalls were aired and I discussed all too briefly, reproduction and fakes. My overview showed that we are at far greater danger of being cheated or deceived in the wider market than ever we are within the antiques and collecting industry. I gave examples from the food industry and from the financial services sector. Now in this chapter I will be taking a close look at fairs and the part they play in adding to the vitality, the optimism, good humour, variety, and at times the seriousness, disappointments and despondency of the industry.

A short history

Whilst there have been fairs and markets for millennia, dealing in all of the commodities of trade, as well as the chaff and the chattels of history, dedicated antiques and collectors fairs and markets are a comparatively recent phenomenon. Fifty years ago they were rare, but go back thirty years, to the 1970s and the industry was beginning to expand rapidly. By the early 1980s, organisers and exhibitors and collectors were to a large extent all smirks and smiles. The frowns and the scowls were still a long way off. These were heady days. There were just enough good fairs around the regions to ensure that long queues formed, four deep at the best venues. The best of the best dealers stock could be stripped from their stands by mid-morning and restocking, particularly for two and three day events was a continuing concern. We even raided our own collections, and sold on our own very special pieces, such was the feeding frenzy in the market at that time. I often regret those very special pieces which are very long since gone, but the experience was important, even decisive and the times memorable. Such was the success of the fairs industry that every Tom, Dick and Harry got in on the act. Good, and of course excellent fairs did continue but the majority of so called antiques and collectors fairs were a travesty. Tom and Dick were beginning to spoil it for Harry.

Inevitably, by the early 1990s much of the fairs scene had become a burgeoning embar-rassment which was to get a good deal worse before it was to ever get better. Three quarters of fairs were poorly organised and even more poorly stocked with so much rubbish and reproduction and new goods that collectors inevitably began voting with their feet. In the next ten years or so the industry was to severely contract. Fortunately the flood of closures washed away much of the flotsam and jetsam. Unfortunately it brought down also a lot of good fairs and good organisers, but many remained. During the first thirty years or so, say from the 1960s, and certainly up to 1994, the old **Shops Act, 1951** held sway and in the main most councils turned a blind eye to Sunday trading at antiques fairs and markets. The industry had Sundays to themselves. The crowds flocked to these novel events, good or mediocre. After all there was little else to do. Supermarkets allowed their vast car parks to get in on the act and giant boot fairs also put their boot into the antiques and collecting industry. During the early 1990s all of the talk in the trade was of a new Act which would legalise the fairs industry. After all a number of regions were at times suffering the scourge of over zealous councils who were, to be fair, having to enforce closure if any member of the public complained. I myself was threatened with a £2,000 fine for organising Sunday fairs and was forced to close down my own events. Many in the trade were looking forward to a new Act which would legalise Sunday trading but we were in the end all completely unprepared for the shopping revolution that was about to descend on the nation. Following the **Sunday Trading Act, 1994** the fairs were actually dealt a massive blow as the huge retail giants opened their doors and Sundays were never to be the same again. Hundreds of years of habit, swept away in one (many people feel) parliamentary moment of madness! Even worse was to follow when the internet, led by *Ebay*, short-circuited the market. This will be discussed in more detail in a later chapter. However despite these two heavy blows the industry has proved to be extremely resilient. The nature of the fairs industry is such that it has many attractions, not the least of which is, that it can offer the opportunity of a hunting trip and a day out. At some of the bigger events you need a couple of refreshment breaks and a lunch break just to get to see most of the stands. Many fairs have about them a vitality and an optimism that is not always present in other areas of the market. They present the opportunity to see new faces and to make new contacts and to view new stock. In the last several years, experienced as well as new organisers have confronted the challenge and new venues have sprung up. Since the millennium closures have continued and the industry has shrunk but it is an indisputable fact that it is now much fitter and healthier, leaner but more resolute and determined and far and away more professional than, say ten years ago. The nature of fairs and their perennial appeal should hopefully ensure a modest period of success and growth for the foreseeable future.

The nature of the fairs industry

The industry provides a magical mix of events. At the higher end of the market there are antiques and fine art fairs where many of the exhibits can be measured in five, six and even seven figure sums. Grosvenor House will serve as an example. At the same level and in the specialist field of ceramics you can pay five figures sums for a cup and saucer at the International Ceramics Fair at The Park Lane Hotel. Well known dealers from all over the world grace these events. Antiques and fine art fairs can be found nationwide and may run from two to five days. Many of the exhibitors are members of dealer associations and operate a strict code of conduct. Some of the larger and some smaller fairs operate a vetting committee who carry out a daily inspection to not only ensure the integrity of the exhibits but also that they reflect the quality of the event. Even genuine antiques, when they are of poor quality and low value will not be permitted. Many antiques and fine art fairs, whilst not strictly providing for a vetting committee, operate a self-vetting system. Here the exhibitors are known to the fairs organisers and are fully conversant with the standards required. Exhibitors at such events would not be expected to display goods that do not match up to the usual high standards required by the organiser. Nothing is 100% and I have seen mislabelled goods even at strictly vetted fairs. These may have been exhibited after the vetting committee's inspection or they may have been overlooked in the first place. I would only occasionally expect these items to be intentionally displayed. Rather they represent a lack of expertise in a particular specialism by the exhibitor. For example I have seen a nineteenth century 'Georgian' glass labelled erroneously as eighteenth. I must stress that spurious goods or misrepresented exhibits at this level of fair are a rare exception. In any event, at fairs of this quality, invoices are always provided and most exhibitors are full time dealers. Both the organisers and the exhibitors will normally provide full consumer protection and in the event of any dispute, buyers will almost certainly have a guarantee that provides much greater security and satisfaction than you are ever likely to find in the new goods sector.

A little further down the pecking order are the better antiques and collectors fairs. These may be regular monthly fairs or even multi-day events, but the quality of stock is well above the average even though much of it may not be antique. Here there will be a good deal of twentieth century collectibles. Many of these organisers insist on good quality and ban reproduction or new goods. Exhibitors who transgress may not get rebooked and will, as often as not, be asked to remove offending goods from their display. I heard many years ago now, the oft told story of a certain 'iron lady' who organised just such an event. On one occasion she found, on her afternoon inspection of the fair, that an exhibitor was displaying reproduction jewellery against her rules. She at once requested that the offending items be removed and told the offender that she would not be rebooking him into any of her events in the future. As the story goes, later in the day, and towards the close of the fair, the now very contrite and apologetic dealer asked the 'iron lady' if she would reconsider. However, she was far too astute to agree, realising that such a show of weakness would compromise her position in the future. In fact the story of her resoluteness echoed around the fairs scene for years to come, thus ensuring that nobody ever tried to break her rules again. Now, I am not saying that such fairs offer full consumer protection, but they are safer places to buy for the beginner than antiques and collectors fairs where there are no rules or guidelines whatsoever. This is not a criticism of such events. They are a natural part of the market. For the intrepid dealer or collector they can provide fertile hunting grounds, as many of the exhibitors are part timers and can occasionally carry stock that has perhaps not been properly researched. Of course they may also carry stock that is overpriced or mislabelled. Errors are rarely deliberate and reflect a lack of knowledge on the part of the exhibitor rather than any deliberate attempt to deceive. And on occasions we are all aware and have perhaps seen, from time to time deliberately fake stock on display. I see no reason why a complaint should not be made to the organiser. After all these people give the industry a bad name and spoil it for everyone.

At the better quality fairs expect to be provided with an invoice for your purchases and this should include a description of the item, as well as an approximate date and the condition in respect of any wear or damage or renovation or restoration. Lower down the pecking order of fairs you may not be offered an invoice or the invoice may be very light on detail. This matters little if you are in full control of the buying situation but if you are buying outside of your expertise then you are advised to ask a few questions before you make a buying decision. In the last chapter I gave an example of just such a case where the buyer ended up with reproduction paintings when he thought he was buying originals, simply for the want of asking a few questions.

If your interests are in good quality antiques or collectibles, say in Georgian drinking glasses, Nathaniel Mills silver, fine classic jewellery or Martin Brothers stoneware then I would expect such dealers and collectors to frequent fairs where they stand a better chance of finding what they are looking for. Always it is a case of horses for courses. The less you specialise the more likely you are to efficiently exploit all levels of the market. I know dealers who have such a wide knowledge of antiques and collectibles as well as the values of a whole range of other secondhand goods that they can profit from boot fairs, fleamarkets and even charity shops. Alternatively if I am collecting Georgian drinking glasses I would not waste my precious time at such events. Rather I will visit specialist glass fairs where there could be hundreds of examples to choose from.

A few years ago, an American lady contacted me and expressed an interest in coming to England to make a career out of buying from boot fairs. She wanted my advice on all of the venues. My advice was to forget it. Better to buy a lottery ticket every week, you will have much more chance of an income! Some dealers will disagree because that is the area of the market in which they operate successfully. I would question that success when they could take their talents further up market and potentially make greater profits. Thirty years of buying and selling has shown me that those antiques which cost a lot of money at the time are those that proved to be the best sellers as well as investments. Always buy the very best you can afford. When I visit antiques fairs I am looking out for and learning about the best pieces in the fair, not the cheapest. When I buy I am looking to buy these better pieces on the grounds that they are at least worthwhile and are the most likely to increase in value over time. If you can buy something for about a £100 that is worth say a £150 it is a better buy than paying £5 for something worth £10. And of course if you continue to buy at the lower end of the market then you will end up short of the essential funds when the occasional, really worthwhile finds cross your path. Regarding boot fairs in general, visit them if you will and certainly if you enjoy them. There is many a bargain to be found across the whole range of household goods and the paraphernalia of humanity in general. But if you are serious about investing in a collection or in household goods or furniture across the board then go as far up market as your pocket can afford. This is the more certain and the more efficient way of building equity into your future. Here is where to find the worthwhile, not rummaging around the junk and the dross and the debris of society where you will need lottery winning luck to succeed. You are not likely to live in the best part of town if you spend hundreds of hours a year mooching around boot fairs. Better to clean windows or cut lawns for a living. You will end up much better off.

The organiser's perspective

The nature of fairs requires that in the main you have to pay an entrance fee. This fee can increase the further upmarket the fair but many of the visitors to fine art and antiques fairs receive free invitations from the organisers or exhibitors because they have a good buying record. For example you buy from an exhibitor and receive a proper invoice giving full details of your purchase(s). This invoice contains the full details of the exhibitor who is usually a full time professional dealer. You have your proof of purchase and nearly always full consumer protection. Many of the organisers who permit our *Antiques Info* Gold Card holders free access to their fairs are in this category. It is not always the nature of the better quality antiques and fine art fairs that they are dependent on an entrance fee to maintain their businesses. On the other hand it is the nature of the market that most antiques and collectors fairs do have to charge an entrance fee, even though this is unpopular with some. I was talking to an acquaintance recently in the north about the fair at Doncaster Racecourse. He was complaining about the entrance fee and the hundreds of exhibitors and had worked out that the organisers were ripping off the public and making a fortune in the process, this with no idea whatsoever of the economics of fair organising. He had no idea that the organiser had to pay a very large rental for the two day venue. He had not even considered the essential costs of the advertising and publicity campaign including costs for leaflets and posters and signage. Nor was he aware of the staff needed to supervise the event, not to mention the general costs of running any business including paying the usual taxes. In fact the entrance fee for many organisers is an essential element in the equation without which the fair could simply not run. When door numbers are down at certain events, due perhaps to a spell of hot weather or local conditions, then certain fairs might prove to be a very uncertain investment. Now whilst fairs organisers do not, in bad times crave our sympathies, they could certainly do with our support. They deserve it. In the main they are the entrepreneurs in our industry who bring colour and variety into our towns and villages.

Chapter V

The Auctions Market

Auctions go back, as do fairs to the beginnings of civilised history, but in both cases the selling of household chattels that possess an antiques or fine art status is a recent development that may be traced back in auction terms to no more than a few hundred years. Auctions themselves were first mentioned as early as 500BC by Herodotus although there can be no doubt that they go back much further. Apparently in Ancient Greece the auction was the only established process through which a daughter could be married off. The prettier and more attractive the girl the higher the price bid and of course the oft told humour surrounds the notion that the plainer and uglier the girl then the greater the dowry that the father would need to add into the equation if he was to successfully marry her off. These early auctions started with the highest offer and worked their way down in price until a successful bid was presented. Today we call this arrangement a Dutch auction. I remember the hilarious and brilliantly funny comedy scene in *Carry on Cleo* where it is the bawdy Roman women who are bidding for the latest batch of men slaves from Britannia, consisting of Kenneth Connor et al and the auction is being conducted by Marcus & Spencerus! In fact Roman auctions were supervised by a magister auctionarium which it would appear is where we derived the modern name.

In modern times and in the United Kingdom art auctions have been held in London since the eighteenth century. Sotheby's was first established in 1744 as a London book dealer and it would appear that Christie's followed in 1766. However it is to the nineteenth century that we must look to trace back the bulk of provincial auctions and many of these were certainly established by the later years. Hence it is now well over a hundred years since the auction as we know it has been offering a range of services to its region, city or town. And these services, although without equal, are now under threat from on-line auctions, which first appeared, led by *Ebay* in 1995. Buying from strictly on-line auctions will be the subject of a later episode in this story. In the meantime let us examine the extensive range of services provided by the 'red brick' auctions, thinned out now, but still very much a vital part of the topography of the town and the economy of the region.

Within the sphere of antiques and collecting there are auctions that operate at almost every level of the market, and they provide outlets for almost every type of goods, from the dross and the debris of society to the very finest of art and antiques. In respect of consumer protection and the pros and cons of the industry, I will tackle that later. For now I am more concerned with looking at those auctions that are more likely to deal with worthwhile antiques and collectibles. Even small town or country auctions may well sell a good smattering of interesting old and antique lots, even though mixed in with a lot of secondhand goods. These auctions are good fun and provide a worthwhile day out. Local humour is frequently the order of the day and you might have a laugh as well as having a bid or two. You never know what might turn up. A few years ago I visited a Sunday country auction, having been tipped off that the sale contained an old drinking glass. This usually means 1950s but this time I had struck lucky as the 'old' glass turned out to be a fine English lead crystal goblet, c1740, in mint condition and down as lot 1. When the auctioneer could muster enough attention he had to work very hard to persuade one of the locals to start the bidding at a rather unflattering £10, and eventually one erstwhile old timer reluctantly agreed. No one else was remotely interested so I offered £20 and that was the end of the bidding. I acquired a glass worth at least £250 at the time, now worth over £500. Generally speaking though, this quality of lot is more readily available at antiques and fine art, or catalogue auctions where the better class of goods have been saved for special sales, held perhaps every two or three months. These may even be two day events where different categories of antiques and fine art are auctioned on different days or separately in the morning or afternoon. Even in the single day auction the lots are grouped into their categories and sold in sections. Typically an auction may commence with a ceramics section, then glass, and move on to silver and jewellery, metalwork, art etc. and conclude with furniture. Some larger provincial auctions even hold specialist sales and are staffed with specialist valuers. At the top end of the market, and in particular in the London auction houses, specialist sales are held on an almost daily basis and cover every worth-while category of collecting. There are also specialist auctions that deal entirely in certain fields, such as coins, stamps, jewellery, books, militaria and even toys, wine or whisky!

Auctions Services

Certainly most antiques and fine art auctions also provide an additional range of services. After all they are not only auctions but as their letterheads tell us they are also valuers. Most regions will certainly have several auctions that fulfil a quite comprehensive role in this respect. Most if not all will certainly allot a half day a week at least to their free valuation days, where members of the public can attend without a prior appointment. Many auctions will also welcome members of the public at almost any time by appointment or without an appointment. Much of their time is also spent visiting homes to look at non-transportable goods or whole house contents. If multiple goods or furniture etc. are taken for auction purposes then the auction house will take responsibility for moving these goods to their saleroom. Additionally such auctions may also provide inheritance tax assessments and probate valuations and may also offer a complete service to executors, solicitors and bank trustees who are involved in administering an estate that includes antiques and fine art. They are also willing to prepare insurance valuations and inventories for the purpose of substantiating any claims in the event of losses resulting from accidents, fire or theft. Auctions are often even prepared to provide preliminary advice, without charge or obligation to clients that are considering a valuation for insurance purposes, capital transfer tax assessment, family division or other purpose.

Auctions Arithmetic

The most important service is the auction itself and it is very important to understand the arithmetic because auctions charge both the vendor and the buyer for this service. These charges are known as the vendor's and the buyer's premiums. This is how auctions make a profit. Ignore television game shows. These skew the way the real market works in the interest of entertainment. These premiums are based on a percentage of the hammer price. They are not fixed charges and therefore the costs to buyers and vendors rises as the hammer price rises. Vendors are pleased to see the hammer price going up because they are continuing to get more for their goods, whilst only paying a percentage of it back to the auction. Buyers on the other hand are not only having to pay more as the hammer price rises but will also have to pay an increasingly greater premium.

Premiums have been rising remorselessly over the last thirty years or so and are now standing at record levels. It's not surprising when you think about it. Certainly in the last twenty years or so prices across the lower and middle markets have stalled and even gone into reverse in some categories of antiques. Auctions turnover is actually down since the late 1980s. For example antique and secondhand furniture has been the basic bread and butter to the auctions industry for as long as the industry has been around. Most auctions in fact are not benefitting from the increased premiums, rather they are being used to keep them afloat. Despite the increased charges closures continue and competition from the Web hasn't helped. Another factor which the antiques and collecting industry and the public at large do not seem to realise is, that unlike other industries, auctions are not able to increase their prices along with inflation. Apart from their marketing strategies they have very little control over hammer prices. They can opt to try to sell only the higher quality antiques and fine art, which will of course be more efficient and bring greater profit. But such goods don't grow on trees and nor can they be ordered from a wholesaler. Or they may opt to sell greater volumes of goods, but they are confronted with the same difficulties. In fact many auctions have found themselves standing still whilst running costs have continued their remorseless rise. This has resulted in generally higher premiums. It is the macro market and a fact of life. I am not going to fully justify these premiums. After all many auctions are resisting the trend and offering as fair a deal as they can manage to their clients whilst others are happy to justify increases. Such is life but some of the increases are larger than they should be. I have seen some basic premiums go from 15% to 17.5% in one fell swoop. In the summer of 2008 *Antiques Info* carried out an *Auctions Survey* and found that 50.2% of auctions are currently charging a buyer's premium of 15%. Only 23.4% of auctions now charge less but worryingly 26.4% are now charging more than 15%. Even more worrying 16.1% of auctions are now charging 17.5%, which, with VAT added takes the premiums over 20%.

Auctions also charge the vendor as well as the buyer. Some auctions charge the vendor less than the buyer, say 10% against 15% but many auctions charge buyer and vendor equally. Now VAT is only paid on the premium, that is on the auctions charges and not on the hammer price. For example if the buyers and vendors premiums are 15% plus VAT then this equates to a rate of 17.625% of the hammer price based on a VAT level of 17.5%. In other words the auction will charge the buyer an additional 17.625% on top of the hammer price and the vendor will only receive the hammer price less 17.625%. The rates charged by auctions can be found in their catalogues or by consulting the relevant auction. The rates may also be complicated by tiered charges where for example you may pay 15% plus VAT buyer's premium on a hammer price of £1,000 but only 10% plus VAT on a hammer price of £30,000. Additionally, although this does not apply to antiques VAT may also be due on the hammer price as well. The lowest buyer's premiums we came across in the **Survey** was

8.5%, which is equal to only 10% including VAT. The highest was 25%, equal to 29.375% including VAT. For vendors there may be further costs related to photographs in the catalogue, storage and insurance. Even excluding these extras the average difference between the real buyer's price and the real vendors price can be more than 35%. This is an important market statement in respect of the relative values of buying and selling antiques at auction. In defence of auctions and the buying and selling of antiques in general this average difference is small when compared to the trading of new goods and will certainly be on average no greater and probably less than the average mark-ups in the retail sector of the antiques and collecting industry.

Estimates and Further Services
The final arithmetic is related to the estimates that appear in auction catalogues. These are designed to help buyers gauge the kind of figures likely to be involved for the purchases of the lots. Each lot is prescribed a price range, say for example £800-£1,000. This estimate does not include the buyer's premium. The lower estimate could represent the reserve price but it will almost certainly not fall below it. The reserve price is that figure, agreed between the vendor and the auction as the minimum hammer price at which the auction agrees to sell the lot. If this figure is not bid then the lot will not be sold. There are also a range of services related to buying at auction which opens up the buying audience beyond the showrooms. If you cannot attend in person you can leave a bid on the books before the auction commences. Similarly many auctions support telephone bidding although many impose a lower limit of, say £200 for example. The auction will phone a few minutes before your lot approaches and then you participate in the bidding as if you were present in the rooms by communicating with their auction representative. It isn't economic to provide telephones for minor lots. This is a worthwhile service and my personal experience shows that this is far more successful than leaving a bid on the books which has little flexibility. To counteract this it is possible to leave a bid in excess of the reserve as the auction should be committed to progressing your bid to the point where your bid becomes successful but you do take the risk of paying more than the lot is worth if you end up in a bidding war. Additionally many auctions have now introduced on-line bidding where prospective buyers register on the auction website and then bid through their PC. A link allows you to follow the progression of the sale as if you were present in the auction room. This system usually depends on a third party company who handle the links and this could mean an additional buyer's premium of say 3% being added to the auction's standard premium. This is all about checking with the auction concerned and reading the terms and conditions to ensure that you understand the charges involved, which you agree before registering. Buying and selling at auction is an important consideration that no collectors or dealers should ignore. It can mean either way that you are operating in a highly professional environment with people who know the market. On the other hand it certainly requires from the dealer or the collector a level of experience and professionalism that will enable them to benefit from such a market.

Not everyone is aware of the additional post sale services on offer. Apart from mailing or arranging carriage on purchases, restoration services may also be available. This could apply to furniture and certainly to repairable goods such as ceramics. You may also be able to get advice on care and maintenance. The specialist jewellery auctioneers, *Fellows &*

Sons of Birmingham take these services very seriously. For example just because a certain ring is not your size this it not necessarily a problem. After the sale the auction will have the ring resized to your requirements, re rhodium-plated if necessary and polished. If the claw setting on the stones are weak then this can be put right. If a diamond has a chip for example, then the auction will find a replacement to the size required and also ensure that the clarity and colour grades are also matched. And then they will insure your purchase to the required amount and send it special delivery. And you do not even have to attend the auction. You can select your prospective purchases from the catalogue or from the on-line website, where the photography is excellent, and bid using any of the various bidding services available. With jewellery you can get a range of classic pieces that are simply not available in the high street.

Consumer Protection

Finally consumer protection. My advice if you are not completely experienced in auctions protocol is to stick to buying and selling through the better antiques and fine art auctions, most of which will belong to trade institutions such as the *Society of Fine Art Auctioneers* (SOFAA) or RICS, *The Royal Institute of Chartered Surveyors*. These operate to a code of conduct and their supporting institution will embrace complaints or investigate malpractices. It's advisable to familiarise yourself with the relevant terms and conditions. It doesn't always have to be 'buyer beware.' For example many auctions will have a rescission clause in their conditions whereby if the buyer is able to prove within say fourteen days that there is an error or omission in a lot description then they will be obliged to rescind the sale and return your money. I wouldn't count on this with all auctions and it is important that the prospective buyer takes responsibility themselves by examining prospective purchases and if necessary consulting the auction if they have any questions.

In the last chapter I discussed the vitality, the optimism and the good humour, as well as the entrepreneurship of the fairs scene. Here it is worthwhile pointing up the professionalism, the industry, the accessibility, multiformity and potency of an auctions industry whose sheer vivacity should always ensure that it commands our attention.

Chapter VI

Antiques Shops and Centres

In Charles Dickens tale, *The Old Curiosity Shop*, the author relates the story of Nell Trent, a beautiful and virtuous young girl. As an orphan she lived with her maternal grandfather in his shop of 'odds and ends'. The actual shop was at 13 Portsmouth Street, in Westminster and remains today as a modern up-market shoe boutique. Dickens apparently knew the shop well. It has an over-hanging upper storey, uneven floor boards and wooden beams and is probably the oldest shop in London, being built in the sixteenth century. It fitted to perfection Dickens' image of *The Old Curiosity Shop* but none the less there is a high degree of assumption in making the link. The original building was made from the timbers of old ships. It survived the *Great Fire* of 1666 and the *Second World War Blitz*. Today it is protected by a preservation order. Here we might also remind ourselves of the much more modern notion of a curiosity or junk shop, being that run with much humour by Jean Alexander (ex Hilda Ogden from *Coronation Street*) playing the sharp, scheming Auntie Wainwright in *Last of the Summer Wine*.

As far as I can tell from Internet research no-one has written anything about the history of antique shops, but then why should they? I cannot even determine when the term was first coined. Clearly in the nineteenth century the term 'curiosity shop' was used for establishments that sold 'strange and rare objects', and 'curios', rather than 'antiques' seems to have been the definition of the times for these 'odds and ends' of history. Certainly the earlier term was in vogue still in 1901, when W R Booth and producer-inventor R W Paul made the early film, *The Haunted Curiosity Shop*. The idea was primitive and relied on an age-old idea that objects may have a life of their own, in this case the various pieces of bric-a-brac on the display shelves of the shop.

Defining the Term 'Antique'

There are dozens of definitions today of the term 'antique', which comes from the Latin 'antiquus', meaning old. As a proper noun, the word 'antiquity' is used to refer to the ancients, that is the people of ancient times and more particularly to the period of ancient Greece and Rome. More broadly it may be considered to be the period of human history from around 3000 BC to the fall of the Roman Empire around 476 AD. But it would appear as we enter the twentieth century that there is a sea change, the term 'antique', previously used only to describe objects from antiquity, is now beginning to be used for art, buildings, furniture, accessories or personal possessions that are over a hundred years old. In fact in 1966 the US Customs Department legalized this definition. But in the last fifty years or so the number of definitions has multiplied, e.g. rugs that are sixty years old are defined as 'antique' and of course once we ascribe any number of years to any definition we have a moving target. Sometimes it would seem that now-a-days that something 'old' is the only qualification needed to call it 'antique'. Alternatively I have discovered a definition that required an item to be hand-made and produced before 1840. In the USA I have found a definition that requires an object to be tangible and more than forty years old, although to be fair it has to be of special historical, cultural, or scientific interest. And I have also noted the term 'antique' ascribed to cars that are twenty five to thirty years old or older.

Antiques Shops and Centres

The period when the term 'antique shop' seems to have entered the language would I suggest have been from about the 1920s onwards, whereas antique centres begin to appear from about 1970. Bennie Gray established *Grays* in a beautiful nineteenth century terra-cotta building in the heart of London's West End in 1977. Today it is home to one of the world's largest and most diverse collections of fine antiques, jewellery, rare books and vintage fashions. Here 200 dealers sell everything from ancient artefacts from 40BC up to twentieth century collectibles. Over thirty years ago Bennie Gray also established *Alfies Antique Market* which also boasts a huge and varied selection of antiques and collectibles. Over the years Alfies has evolved to become home to the best dealers of twentieth century design as well as vintage fashion and antiques. And it is probably true to say that, as the wheels of fashion have turned towards a growing interest in the twentieth century, that the terms 'antiques shop' or 'antiques centre' is not intended to be misleading in the sense of the hundred year rule, but rather reflects the latest trends which ensure an eclectic mix of art, antiques and collectibles from any period. As one antiques centre owner told me recently, if she hadn't encouraged her dealers to move their stock more towards the twentieth century and particularly towards relatively modern collectibles, then she wouldn't have survived!

The 1970s

When I first took an interest in antiques and collecting the retail industry was represented in the main by the antiques shop, small and singly owned or rented. Some of course, especially in tourist towns and villages were in primary locations. Often almost all the high street had become antique shops, such as Brasted, or Sandgate in Kent. This is still the case today in certain cities, towns and regions, and the better end of the market is maintained by their connections to national or regional, or even village trade associations. Petworth in West Sussex is a typical example of a famous village with antiques associations. But there was always antiques and collectibles to be found at every level of the market. I remember in the 1970s and 1980s one of my favourite haunts was in Stockport when the dozens of antique shops, in a secondary location admittedly, could occupy a good day's hunting at least. Many readers will remember that the good thing about those days was that the single proprietors couldn't know about everything so a specialist dealer or collector could more easily find bargains. I specialised in Georgian ceramics and drinking glasses and most shop owners were weak in these areas. Georgian coffee cans could be had for a pound or two as could eighteenth century/early nineteenth century blue and white and I would pick up occasionally opaque and air twist glasses for a song. Profits were usually modest. In the end of course dealers have their own considerable costs in selling on, not least is the cost of all of the driving! However the occasional lucky find was always a bonus. On one occasion I paid the asking price of a £100 for a pair of Bristol blue decanters, minus a stopper, which I later sold for £1,200, but this was only after I had paid Wilkinsons, the famous glass restorers formerly of Catford, £200 to have an original eighteenth century stopper ground to fit.

The 1980s

The 1980s were the last of the good times for the retail trade and the dealer working in the ways I have described. In a previous edition I have already explained how the burgeoning fairs industry began to collapse, but we must also remember that the fairs industry played its part in weakening the retail sector. It was much more comfortable to stroll around in the warmth of indoor venues where there could be up to a 100 stands on view than plodding the wintery streets of Wigan or Stockport on a bleak January Tuesday. Additionally of course the fairs scene could also be populated with a percentage of 'beginner dealers' who were learning the trade and bargains could always be found. Nothing is forever of course and the wheels of fashion will turn remorselessly. The mass interest in collecting subsided and by the late eighties and early nineties the retail sector was in retreat and the country was also in recession. Another factor, never attributed to the collapse of the retail industry before, was beginning to make its mark.

The Uniform Business Rate

The middle and lower ends of the retail industry had usually resided in the more secondary and even tertiary positions in the towns. Of necessity these small businesses couldn't afford most high street rates. However as rates in general climbed and in particular the uniform business rate, the junk shops (I use the term affectionately) simply couldn't survive. And the wholesale closures of small family businesses in isolated locations or in the shopping malls of towns throughout the country, was not restricted to the antiques trade alone. Small family retail businesses of all kinds simply couldn't afford to trade because of the higher overheads. Thus began the age of the charity shops, whose special status and free stock and volunteer staff ensured that they at least could enjoy high street status, but at the expense of other small businesses. Our small town in Kent, at its peak, had seven charity shops on the high street whilst other small businesses struggled in more secondary positions. In the 1990s we began to lose some of these. One was a wonderful DIY shop and nothing to do with antiques. You could buy only four screws if that was all you needed, or have a piece of wood or hardboard cut to size. Mr Hurley succumbed when the turnover in his shop could no longer pay the overheads of the business. Bitterly he related to me one day, how a parking attendant, making two or three passes up and down his one-way street in a day issuing tickets at £25 a go, could turn over more business in a day, than he could make in a week in his shop! Additionally I do not need to remind readers how town centres and small retail businesses in particular have been blighted by out-of-town shopping malls.

The National Parking Meter Scheme

Regarding the new parking regime that has been rolled out across the country, I've listened to all sides of the debate. Councillors will argue that the new regime prevents drivers permanently, or perhaps for several hours at a time taking up spaces that could allow a continuous stream of shoppers throughout the day, paying for their 30 minutes at a time.

We conducted our own straw poll which suggests that the threat of fines and stress caused by the worry of being late back to parking meters more than ensures that most surveyed insist that they will park anywhere they can rather than pay and worry! And in secondary or tertiary positions, often in residential streets, the meters have ensured they remain virtually empty of cars, which are now clogging up other residential streets without meters, and some of these are busy thoroughfares. Parking areas with meters have been placed in the most incongruous positions, such as opposite 'T' junctions where there should be double yellow lines, causing traffic build ups. Meanwhile shop owners can see no benefits whatsoever from the national metering scheme.

Sunday Trading Act, 1994 and beyond

Of course in 1994 along came the Sunday Trading Act, blighting the town centres still further as millions shifted their shopping days to Sundays, not to mention the effect on church attendances. Even worship was to be marginalised. However it wasn't to be all doom and gloom as already mentioned. By the 1970s the antiques centres were beginning to spring up and these have proliferated in the last twenty years but there have also been closures. I rented my first room in an antiques centre in 1976. One of the earliest was Hemswell Antiques Centre, just off the A15 in Lincolnshire and only a few miles from the famous Dambusters aerodrome at RAF Scampton. Hemswell is big and was one of the first centres in the region. It has unlimited parking. One of the main advantages of many of the UKs antiques centres is their accessibility. Nobody in any event would open an antiques centre unless they had ensured ample parking for dealers who are loading and unloading and for customers who may also have loading needs. This is why the out-of-town shopping centres have the advantage over the high streets. They provide almost unlimited parking spaces. Parking space is the key to successful trading and the boot of the car is the key to shopping expeditions. Antique centres can also provide a huge diversity of stock that would simply be beyond the single antique shop. In centres dealers can usually rent anything from a small cabinet for as little as £20 or £30 a month right up to large furniture spaces. They are a godsend to dealers, who now do not have to worry about the viability of owning or renting a shop in a difficult trading position. Today's retail dealers are much more versatile. Typically they might keep stock in more than one antiques centre in their region and in addition stand at a number of antiques fairs. Stock unsold from fairs can be put back or moved into antiques centres. Wise dealers and collectors visiting a region on a buying trip know that they have to be aware of the dates, particularly of major fairs in the region.They have to anticipate when the best stock may be removed from the static shop or centre situation for display at fairs. In other words it would be unwise to plan a buying trip to shops and antiques centres, particularly in the northern region, in the days before the showground events at Swinderby or Newark. Even auctions have to be wary about clashing with the big fairs events because the trade would be missing in their droves!

The larger antiques centres can provide a good day out and many like Hemswell have their own tea rooms and even restaurants. Timing is important and you are better visiting after large regional events, when new or recent purchases may be more available. However dealers in antiques centres can be adding or removing stock at any time and prospective buyers should visit regularly to get the feel or the flavour of the local action. There are certain disappointing features about antiques centres. Usually cabinet holders are absent and you can't always ask questions about items of stock that might interest you. Frequently labels in cabinets are frustratingly upside down and you can't read the description or the price. Staff will come and open cabinets but this can sometimes mean returning to the reception area to summon assistance and this can be irritating if you are short of time. Centres are different from fairs in that you cannot always discuss your prospective purchase with the vendor and invoices are made out by third parties at reception who are not always able to answer all of the questions you wish to ask, nor can they commit themselves to ensuring that the invoice contains the three essential ingredients in respect of secondhand goods, that is the approximate age, the description of the item and its condition, details that at times can be absent from labels. Labelling can of course be misleading because of the dealers lack of knowledge or occasionally they could be deliberately misleading but this is rarely the case. The worst scenario is where there is no description whatsoever and the label carries only a price. In certain categories of antiques this might be a problem but it shouldn't be if you are buying in an area of your own expertise. Unfortunately it can sometimes be the case that labels are deliberately thin or even void of any description. Readers will remember that in an earlier chapter I quoted the actual case of two reproduction paintings that were only marked with a price, and a relative of mine bought them thinking they were about a hundred years old. As he had recently bought a reproduction glass rummer from the same antiques centre thinking it to be 200 years old he was not amused when I explained about the paintings and as a result lost confidence in buying from that antiques centre. This is wrong and such goods should be plainly marked for what they are, as it is entirely reasonable that beginners or novices should expect old paintings in an antiques centre, not new masquerading as old.

In general however the antiques trade is much more trustworthy than the new goods sector, but I believe there is more work to be done by antiques centre managers in setting higher standards, which I believe will pay off. At least the antiques sector does not deal in the heavy marketing employed by the food giants and other sectors, particularly in relation to prices and their so called special offers, where the mathematical manipulations, in the interests of pushing the notion of the bargain is frequently unethical and at times downright immoral. The best thing about the antiques and collecting industry is that in the main, and compared to the new goods sector it is, apart from a minority of dealers, as honest as the day is long. If I were to 'fault' or rather grumble about antiques centres as such, it is that, certainly from a dealers perspective, and perhaps also from a collector's point of view, that such is the diversity of dealer knowledge, which of course is quite frequently and naturally shared, that finding the absolute bargain is much more difficult than it used to be! If this though is the worst that can be said about antiques centres they have my blessing as a collector and my admiration if I am to don my dealer's hat! This can of course work both ways though, in which case it is to everyone's benefit.

Chapter VII

Buying on the internet

The nature of the internet

The influence of the internet on many people's lives cannot be overestimated and this is particularly relevant to the antiques and collecting industry. Whilst the astute collector or dealer will continue to explore and exploit the traditional markets in all of their forms, 'switched on' people will be making very efficient use of their time plumbing the limitless depths of the **World Wide Web**. Freed from the shackles of time and distance, or miles-per-hour, and night and day, and opening and closing hours, they may sit at their windows of opportunity, their portals to the stars and view their own universe of choice or their particular microcosm of interest. What a pity therefore that all of the talk and all the debate and the controversy should centre on what has been described as 'the biggest boot fair of all time', *Ebay*! Only recently a reader has complained that he was sick of being 'done' on this famous, or some might say, infamous website. However *Ebay* is little different to any market in the history of humanity, except for its size. We might just as well find fault with the financial services sector of the economy, or the Government or the transport network or television, but in the end we will find there is good and bad in everything and *Ebay* are no worse than any other large institution with arbitrary principles and self-facing terms and conditions. Rather it is up to us in the sense that it is what we make of the market rather than what the market makes of us, that will count in the end.

This said the internet provides for almost every conceivable need. On our own website at **www.antiques-info.co.uk** we have concentrated on providing information. After all we offer a multimedia service. Here subscribers can gain access to a range of information databases. The most popular is our database of sales results across all categories of antiques and collecting in recent years. Here users can select a particular category of collecting, such as *Ceramics*, and then sub search for their field of interest, such as *Doulton*, and then check out hundreds and sometimes thousands of illustrated results of sales. Or if your interest is glass then you can check out the market for *Whitefriars* or even look specifically at the prices for *Drunken Bricklayer* vases in recent years. Anyone who is a serious dealer or collector can access our full range of services for as little as a pound a month, an investment, not a cost! We also provide information and advice and valuations. In other words, and briefly, we provide not only a huge research facility but also do research on behalf of our subscribers when they need it. There are other websites which have results databases such as **www.antiquestradegazette.com** Readers may also check out **www.invaluable.com**. I have read that there are a million or more websites that operate in the field of antiques and collecting and I can believe it! And most are in the retail business, an endless high street of never ending shop widows, but now only our fingers do the walking and never our feet! The virtual world is now the most important milestone in the history of shopping! And not only do they display their goods, but they also provide multimedia communication links with the world so that you can discuss prospective purchases or just get some further information. I have heard that some internet shoppers consider their own anonymity a blessing and certainly a distinct advantage, but I have never subscribed to this opinion. Personally a face to face with the seller and a face to face with the goods takes some beating but I buy more on the web today than I buy in a retail situation because it is efficient in every respect. I am able to find prospective purchases on the web on a regular basis that I would never find in several lifetimes of having to physically search. Many of these are the result of emails from auctions who know what I am seeking and email me when lots that may be of interest come along. Years ago we had no choice. One might travel a thousand miles and visit dozens of shops in a couple of weeks of hunting. Today I can view more stock in an hour and view only the stock that I might want to buy.

Let me illustrate this with some examples. Say I am interested in collecting antique and vintage teddy bears. Let me now go into **Google** and search. I am overwhelmed with the choice of websites that I may visit. As my interest is only in old bears I will select a promising site but there are many that I could choose. In this case I have selected a site called **Lucky Bears Limited** and the home page allows me to click on antique and vintage bears for sale. There are 48 bears on this site and there are multiple and excellent quality images of each bear. For example I have clicked on a rare *Nickle Nackle* teddy bear by Rudolf Haas, c1930. There is a full description. He is seventeen inches tall and is priced at £1,475 although in the secondhand market I would expect that there might be some negotiation on the price. There are bears on this site in all price ranges and to suit every pocket. With each bear I can also bring up a *Condition Report*, as you can on many auction and retail sites. In this case I can read that this bear has *some balding......his beige feet pads are replacements......* and he has a small string on his chest.....*which appears to be the remnants of the original label.*

Changing categories, let me now search for *Nantgarw* and *Swansea* porcelains, a very important area of collecting for the Welsh. As expected there are less websites to choose from but I have selected a site called **The Welsh Connection**. This is interesting because this excellent website includes a written history of these important and famous Welsh porcelains. Similarly on my own personal website at **www.georgianglass.com** I have included several essays about the history of Georgian glass in general and in particular on identifying Georgian glass. Back to **The Welsh Connection** and I can view the stock of *Nantgarw* and *Swansea* porcelains. Each piece is meticulously described and there are multiple images. All of the stock is priced and there is a full range of contact details.

As a final example let me look for antiquarian booksellers. Now there are many sites but to cut a very long story short I was able to sub-search one particular site, and come up with results for *Robert Burns*, *Sir Winston Churchill* and *Ian Flemming*, et al, and rather interestingly, *Original Artwork* which is all the rage at the present time. Incidentally many of the antiques centres or trade supermarkets also have websites. For example I have just keyed in **Hemswell Antique Centre** which is just north of Lincoln and one of the biggest in the country. I know Rob Miller, the owner is very proud of his website. Here there is a comprehensive list on the home page of the various categories of antiques and collecting.

I clicked on *glass* and was able to view a good selection of their current stock. Communications are easy, buying is simple and postage costs are reasonable. The main point here is that although I know the Centre well I now live about 200 miles away so regular visits are simply not an option. The world has indeed, opened up.

I hope that the foregoing has given any beginners a good flavour of the Web. However for those that haven't been brought up with a computer my task here is also to engender in readers a trust in the Web. Today there are so many stories going around about bad reports that we can be forgiven if we do not want to place any trust in on-line buying. The truth is of course that the vast majority of traders and dealers on the web are as honest as the day is long and as long as you use your common sense, as you very much have to practice in the real world then you are not going to go far wrong. In the end we will all of us visit those retail outlets or restaurants or garages or go on holidays where we trust those who provide these services. The bottom line is in fact that we will always be willing to operate within our own comfort zones. The next part of this story will hopefully extend your comfort zone by discussing the law in general related to buying goods and the law in particular related to buying on the internet, where card payments and branded payment collection networks like *Pay Point* and *Paypal* come into play.

The law and the internet

To ensure that I am quoting the latest information related to buying over the internet, I've logged on to **www.adviceguide.org.uk,** the website run by the *Citizens Advise Bureau* and sub searched for 'buying over the internet.' In addition I have also researched the **Which?** commentary at **www.which.co.uk** Much of the following is therefore a paraphrase of the general advice given on these important consumer websites.

When you buy goods over the internet from a UK based company, you have the same rights as if you had bought them from a shop. The laws say the goods must:

1. Match their description. This means they must be as described by the seller. This includes any description on the label. For example, if a vase is described as being made of porcelain, it cannot be constructed of any other material. In most circumstances, it also means that the vase must conform to any advertising claims made about it.

2. It must be of be of satisfactory quality. This means the goods must meet the standards that any reasonable person would expect. This includes their condition, appearance and finish. The goods must also be fit for their purpose, which includes what you would normally expect from the goods in question and also anything that you have specifically pointed out for the seller. For example, if you were buying a pair of antique grape scissors and had asked whether they were in working condition, then they must do so, otherwise the seller would be at fault. In respect of secondhand goods, I have pointed out on numerous occasions in this study that an invoice or bill should not only state what the object is but also give an indication of its age and its condition. Unspecified restoration and a failure to point out that an item masquerading as an antique, is either a reproduction, or new, are common problems in the antiques and collecting industry.

In addition the *Citizens Advice Bureau* tell us, if the seller sells the goods in the course of a business (rather than a private sale), a criminal offence may have been committed if the goods are unsafe, or their description or price is false to a material degree. If you feel this may be the case you should report the matter to **Consumer Direct** on 0845 404 0506.

In addition you may have rights when you buy over the internet, including the right to clear information before you decide to buy, including the name of the seller and the price of the goods, including any extras like VAT or delivery charge. If you pay money before delivery, the seller must also give you their full postal address. This information must be written and can be in a letter, fax, e-mail or on the website; and you have the right to cancel your order up to seven working days after receipt of the goods and get your money back, although you might have to pay for their return. You cannot cancel if the goods were made to order, perishable, newspapers, or software, audio or video recordings which have been unsealed. You may also not be able to cancel if you have a service (for example the installation of a fitted kitchen) which you agree to have completed before the seven day cancellation period is up; and have the goods delivered within 30 days of your order unless you and the seller agreed otherwise. If the seller later realises they cannot deliver within this time, they must tell you and give you the option of cancelling and getting a full refund. You also have the right to protection from fraud if you pay by a credit, debit or store card. If someone makes dishonest or fraudulent use of your payment card, you can cancel the payment and the card issuer must refund all the money to your account. You must inform the company that issues the card as soon as you suspect that someone else is using the card. These rights do not apply, for example, when buying goods at an on-line auction. If you used your credit card to pay for the goods and they cost more than £100 and less than £30,000, the credit card company may have equal liability, even if the company is not based in the UK. When you buy goods over the internet, your rights depend on what the law says in the country where the company is based. If the seller is based in a European Union country, you may have similar rights as if the company is UK based. If there is anything misleading, indecent or dishonest you can also complain to the *Advertising Standards Authority*.

What to do if the goods don't arrive, or are faulty
If the goods aren't delivered by the agreed date or within thirty days, you have the right either to cancel the order and get your money back, or ask for a replacement. If the goods are damaged when they are delivered or are substantially different from their description on the website, you are entitled to ask for a full refund, including the cost of all postage and packaging. Faulty goods are not subject to the return time limit, but you must contact the seller within a reasonable period. If the goods are faulty and you return them promptly you don't have to agree to a replacement or repair. If you have had the goods some time before you notice the fault, you would normally have lost your right to a refund but would be entitled to have the goods replaced or repaired. The repair should be carried out within a reasonable time and must restore the goods to a satisfactory condition. If the goods cannot be replaced or repaired, you would be entitled to a refund or the cost of buying the goods elsewhere. If you have had the goods some time, the seller may be entitled to offer you less than the purchase price to take into account the use you have had from them.

Compensation
You may be entitled to compensation if:
1. The contract has been broken (breach of contract), for example the goods don't match their description or are not of satisfactory quality or fit for their purpose; or
2. You have incurred additional expenses or inconvenience because of breach of contract

or negligence, for example, there is an electrical fault on a toaster you buy over the internet and this starts a fire, damaging other property; or

3. Someone has been injured because the goods were unsafe. In such circumstances you should contact *Consumer Direct* on 0845 404 0506 before returning the goods to the seller. Always take legal advice before deciding whether to accept an offer of compensation for personal injury; or

4. The seller made a false statement about the goods to persuade you to buy; or

5. You have accepted a repair which has turned out to be unsatisfactory.

The amount of compensation you are entitled to will depend upon the seriousness of the breach of contract and could include the cost of replacing the goods or repair.

How to solve your problem

Once you have decided what your rights are, contact the seller. The following steps should help solve your problem:

1. Stop using the goods.

2. Find your proof of purchase. A credit card statement, copy of your email order or confirmation you received from the seller will do.

3. If someone has been injured or you think that the trader may have committed a criminal offence, contact *Consumer Direct* on 0845 404 0506 when you discover the fault. If you ring or email, make a note of what was said. Follow it up with a letter and enclose copies of your proof of purchase. Explain what the problem is calmly but firmly and ask for what you want, a refund, replacement, repair or compensation.

4. If you cannot contact the seller, for example, because the email or website address has become unavailable, you could ask your internet service provider for help tracking down the seller or by posting a message in a relevant newsgroup or chat room.

5. Write to the owner/manager of the company repeating your complaint and the steps taken to resolve it. Say you are giving them fourteen days to resolve the problem after which you will consider taking legal action. Send the letter by recorded delivery with a copy to the head office of the company, if there is one. Keep copies of all your letters and a note of any phone conversations you have in connection with the problem.

6. If the seller doesn't respond, refuses to do anything, or makes a final offer you are unwilling to accept, your only other choice is to go to court. Remember court is your last resort. Before starting court action you need to consider whether you have sufficient evidence. You also need to find out if the seller is solvent. It is not worth suing someone who has no money. If the company is not UK based, it may be very difficult to take legal action or enforce any award. (although you may be able to take proceedings against a credit company alone if the price of the goods was over £100) If you have lost money buying things on the internet, don't waste money on a case you can't win. There are organisations that deal with complaints about internet sellers.

Advertising Standards Authority (ASA)

UK websites are considered to be adverts and therefore have to observe the British Codes of Advertising, Sales Promotion and Direct Marketing, which say that adverts must be legal, decent, honest and truthful. It may also be a criminal offence if the website describes goods in a misleading way in order to sell them. The contact number is 020 7492 2222.

Citizens Advice Bureau

Citizens Advice Bureaux give free, confidential, impartial and independent advice to help solve problems. To find your nearest CAB, including those that give advice by e-mail, click on nearest CAB, or look under C in your phone book.

Buying on Internet Auction Sites

This information applies to England, Wales, Scotland and Northern Ireland and is about your rights when you buy goods from a website calling itself an internet auction site. It does not cover your rights if you are selling goods through one of these sites. It applies only if you are buying goods on an internet auction site from a seller based in the UK or EU. If the seller is based elsewhere, different rules may apply, even if the internet site itself is based in the UK or the EU. It is important to know where the seller is based so that you can find out which rights apply. To find out about buying from sellers based in other EU countries, visit the website of *UK European Consumer Centre* at **www.ukecc.net**, or phone 08456 040503.

Buying goods on internet auction sites has become a very popular way to shop. A wide range of goods is available for sale from a large number of sellers, in a number of different ways. These sites may call themselves auction sites, but they don't operate in the same way as traditional auctioneers, and they don't have the same responsibilities. When you buy something from an internet auction site, you are usually buying from the seller, not the site, and it is the seller you will need to complain to if something goes wrong. The seller could be a private individual, or a business trader. It is important to know which, as this will affect your rights. As a rule, you will have more rights if the seller is a business trader.

There are different types of sales available on internet auction sites. Some are auction-style sales involving bidding for items. Others, for example *Buy-it-now* on *Ebay,* aren't auction sales at all. Your rights will depend on the type of sale you buy from. They will also depend on whether any extra protection is available through the terms and conditions of the site, or through the method of payment you have used.

If you buy goods on an internet auction site and the seller is a business trader, you have at least as many rights as if you had bought the goods in a shop and sometimes more. This means the goods must again be of satisfactory quality and match the description given on the website. They should be free of any faults, including minor ones. They should be of the same quality and last as long as a reasonable person would expect. You must also be able to use the goods for the purpose that you would normally expect of this type of product.

If there is something wrong with the goods, you should complain to the seller. Depending on how serious the problem is and how quickly you make your complaint, you may be able to: return the goods and get your money back, get a free repair done, get a replacement for the goods, get some of your money back or claim compensation. The seller should pay for any postage costs involved in sending goods back or in getting them repaired.

As well as your normal shopping rights, you also have some extra rights when you buy goods online from a business trader. This includes the right to be given the name and address of the business trader before you place your order. You may also have some additional rights because you have bought something from a trader without having face-to-face contact with them. Buying this way is known as distance selling. The most important extra right you have when you buy online from a business trader in one of these ways, is the right to a 'cooling off' period. This means you can cancel your order if you change your mind about wanting the goods. You can do this within seven working days after the day the goods are delivered. You can cancel your order within this period, even if there's nothing wrong with the goods and get all your money back, including the postage charge. The trader must tell you that you have the right to a seven day cooling off period *before* you place your order. If they don't, the cooling off period will start when they tell you in writing about your right to cancel, or three months after the goods are delivered, whichever comes first.

If you want to cancel your order, you must do this in writing. The trader must return your money within thirty days. You may have to pay for returning the goods if the trader has told you about this before you bought them. If you do have to pay for returning your goods, make sure you choose a postal service with enough insurance to cover any loss or damage. When you buy on-line from a business trader, the trader must make sure you receive your goods within thirty days. If you don't you have the right to cancel and get a refund. You might be able to get extra compensation on top. When you buy goods from a business trader, it is the responsibility of the trader if the goods are lost or damaged before delivery. You don't have to buy extra postal insurance to protect your goods against loss or damage.

Using your Credit Card to buy goods
If you used your credit card to buy something from a business trader on an internet auction site, you may be able to make a claim against the credit card company instead of the trader if there is something wrong with the goods. This could be useful where the trader has gone out of business or has no money to compensate you. To be able to claim against the credit card company, the goods must have cost more than £100 and less than £30,000. If you paid by credit card it may also be possible for you to get a payment reversed.

Buying Secondhand goods
When you buy secondhand goods from a business trader on an internet auction site, you have the same rights as if they were new. However, if there is a problem, you will need to take into account the price you paid for the goods when deciding whether you expect the trader to do anything about it. You shouldn't necessarily expect the goods to be of perfect quality, and your expectations of their performance may be lower. Under certain, limited circumstances, it's possible to lose some of your normal shopping rights when you buy secondhand goods through an internet auction site. This could happen if you are offered the chance to view the goods in person. Although this is rare, it can sometimes happen.

Buying from a Private Individual
When you buy something on an internet auction site from a private individual, you have few rights. You can't complain if the goods aren't of satisfactory quality or fit for the purpose you bought them. Also, you don't have the right to cancel your order, or any of the other extra rights you get when you buy on an internet auction site from a business trader. However, you do still have the right to complain to the seller if your goods don't match the description they've given on the website. This applies to secondhand as well as new goods. If the goods don't match the description, you may be entitled to compensation from the seller. But you might need to go to court, and even if you win your case, the seller might

not have enough money to pay you. When you buy goods from a private seller, you may not be able to make a claim against them if the goods are damaged or lost before delivery. However, if the seller has offered you postal insurance and you have accepted, they will be expected to make a claim on the insurance on your behalf.

Site Protection Schemes

Some internet sites have a protection scheme. These schemes can deal with problems such as non-delivery of goods or goods not matching their description. They can be useful if you want to avoid going to court, or the seller is from overseas, so it's worth checking if you can make a claim under one of these schemes.

However, you need to bear in mind the following:

1. You may only have a very short period of time in which to make a claim.
2. There may be several types of problem which the scheme doesn't cover.
3. The amount of money you can claim on the scheme might be limited.
4. The number of claims you can make on the scheme may be limited.

You may have to try other options for solving your problem first, for example, making a claim through your credit card provider, if you paid by credit card. To make a claim, you will also need to have followed the auction-site rules, policies or user agreement. This means that you won't be able to claim if you dealt with the seller directly through email instead of through the site.

Dispute Resolution Schemes

Some internet sites offer a dispute resolution service. This is a scheme which will help you and the seller try to reach an agreement. Some schemes involve the services of trained mediators and will charge a fee. It's important to remember that you might not always get what you want when you use one of these schemes. Even if the seller agrees to pay you some money, there may not be a way of making sure they do pay up.

Payment Protection Schemes

Many payments for things bought on internet auction sites are now made through special payment services, such as *Paypal*. *Paypal* is an online payment account and has become one of the most popular ways to pay for goods on online auction website *Ebay*. Rather than give your bank or credit card details directly to the retailer, you pay money into your *Paypal* account and use this to pay for your items instead. *Paypal* was bought by *Ebay* in 2002. Payment services will collect your money and won't release it to the seller until you have received your goods. This has clear security advantages when dealing with private sellers and retailers that you have not dealt with before. It also speeds up payments for goods, compared to paper-based options such as cheques and postal orders. The vast majority of buyers and sellers on *Ebay* are genuine and the goods they are offering match their descriptions. However in any market place there are bound to be rogue traders, or those who are willing to stretch the truth when describing the goods they are selling in order to secure a better price. These services can be useful, but offer very different levels of protection for your money. Look at the terms and conditions to find out what the scheme does or doesn't do. What you really need to find out when buying through *Paypal* is the amount of protection their scheme gives you, particularly if your goods fail to arrive or they are faulty. I have checked the **www.which.co.uk** website and they don't think that *Paypal* gives enough protection in these circumstances. However they do protect against ID fraud. One weakness suggested by *Which?* is that Section 75 of the *Consumer Credit Act* doesn't apply. This is related to when you use your credit card to make a purchase that is between a £100 and £30,000 and where, if the item isn't delivered or there is something wrong with it, you can make a claim against the retailer or your credit card provider.

When you use an online payment service, you may find that your payments are not fully protected in some circumstances, for example, if you are dealing with sellers from overseas. You may also find that you are not protected if you did not complain within the time limits, which are sometimes very short, or you entered into a deal with the seller outside the internet site. You can certainly get extra protection if you pay by credit or charge card. Many card networks, including credit cards and charge cards, operate chargeback arrangements. This means that, in some circumstances, you may be able to get a payment reversed. Check with your credit or charge card provider whether they operate chargeback arrangements. A *Visa* debit card is covered by *Visa's* debit card chargeback scheme which allows you to claim money back if goods do not arrive, arrive damaged or are not as described. There is no similar scheme covering *Maestro* debit cards but you can apply for a chargeback if goods ordered from overseas do not arrive. Chargeback time limits can be tight and the schemes may not cover all types of claim. Where they operate, they will apply to payments made to overseas as well as UK sellers.

Going to Court
If you have tried everything else but still got nowhere, you could think about making a claim against the seller in court. Going to court should be a last resort. If you haven't made a genuine effort to sort out your problem before starting court action, even if you win your case the court may reduce your compensation. Before you go to court, you need to think about whether you have enough evidence. It will be up to you to prove your case. There is no guarantee that you will win your case and you may end up losing money. You also need to find out if the seller has enough money to pay your claim. It is not worth suing someone who has no money.

What to do if you can't trace the seller
If you aren't able to trace the seller, contact the website. The site may be able to give you the seller's details. There is nothing in law which prevents them from doing this. However, they don't have to give you the seller's details if they don't want to. If the seller appears to operate their own website with their own domain name, it may be possible to find out how to contact them by searching on a 'Who is' search engine, such as **www.samspade.org**, **www.truewhois.com** or **www.nominet.org.uk** (UK domains only).

What to do if fraud is involved
If you suspect that fraud is involved, in England, Wales and Scotland, you should report it to *Consumer Direct* on 08454 04 05 06 or online at **www.consumerdirect.gov.uk**. *Consumer Direct* can also give you advice about what you can do. You can also report fraud to the police. You can find contact details for local police stations and report some things online at: **www.online.police.uk**. In Northern Ireland, you should report fraud to

Consumerline on 0845 6006262 or online at **www.consumerline.org**. To contact the police, go to: **www.psni.police.uk**. You should be aware that there may be very little that *Consumer Direct*, *Consumerline* or the police can do.

Look out especially for sellers who invite you to trade outside the internet site by offering to sell you something for the same or a lower price. Watch out also for fake payment protection schemes which fail to pass your money on to the seller and beware of people who contact you when you are the losing bidder at an online auction, offering to sell you a similar product. This is likely to be a fraudster. They will insist on payment through an online payment scheme and then fail to deliver the goods. Beware also of items which cost a lot more than you think they're worth. Sellers can get people they know to put in false bids so that they can get a higher price. You should also report suspected fraud to the internet auction site. There are a number of ways in which they can penalise someone who is acting outside the rules of the site, including suspending their account.

If you suspect that a seller is a business trader pretending to be a private individual, you should complain to *Consumer Direct* on 0845 404 0506. *Consumer Direct* is a telephone and online consumer advice service, supported by the *Office of Fair Trading* and local authority *Trading Standards* services. The advice and information is free, but telephone calls to *Consumer Direct* are charged at 0845 prices. *Consumer Direct* is currently available in England, Scotland and Wales. Website: **www.consumerdirect.gov.uk**

ConsumerLine is run by the *Trading Standards* service and *The General Consumer Council* and offers advice to consumers in Northern Ireland. Tel: 0845 600 6262. Website: **www.consumerline.org**

The *Office of Fair Trading* (OFT) is a government department which oversees trading practices to make sure that they are fair and that customers are protected. The OFTs website has useful information about, amongst other things, your shopping rights, internet fraud and buying safely online at: **www.oft.gov.uk**.

Getsafeonline's website has useful information about how to buy safely online at: **www.getsafeonline.org.uk**.

The UK European Consumer Centre provides help in sorting out problems with traders based in other European Union countries. You can find more information at: **www.ukecc.net**, or phone 08456 040503.

Econsumer.gov is a website which allows you to report complaints about sellers based in some non-European Union countries. The website address is: **www.econsumer.gov**.

Editor's Note: My acknowledgement and thanks to **www.adviceguide.org.uk**, the website of the *Citizens Advise Bureau* and to *Which?* at **www.which.co.uk**. Much of the information in these pages was taken from these two important consumer websites.

Contents

CW00601688

Safety

Your baby depends upon you entirely for safety. Think ahead and avoid the dangers.

- Babies need to have their necks and heads carefully supported at all times.

- Lay your baby down to sleep on his back unless your doctor advises otherwise.

- Never use pillows, duvets or cot bumpers; they could cause suffocation.

- The safest place for your baby to sleep is in a cot in your room for the first six months.

Safety

● Don't risk strangulation. Avoid dressing your baby in clothes with ribbons, draw strings or braces and keep cots away from window blinds with dangling cords.

● Change nappies on the floor or keep everything close by and don't leave for a second.

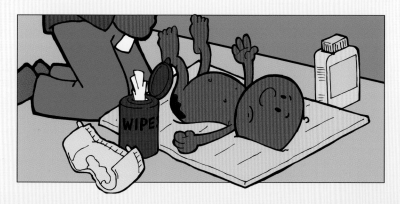

● Remember; **NEVER** leave your baby on a raised surface, you can't be sure how soon he or she will learn to roll over.

● Don't smoke anywhere near your baby. Better still don't smoke at all.

● Keep hot drinks out of the way of your baby.

Do not pass hot drinks across your baby.

Safety

- Keep small objects well out of reach.

- Check that toys are suitable for babies and have no broken bits, sharp edges or loose parts.

● Always use the straps in prams and baby seats.

● Use a rear facing baby seat when travelling in a car.

Never use a rear facing baby seat in the front of a car with a passenger airbag.

Healthy Eating

● Healthy eating is important for you as well as your baby. A balanced diet will help to keep you fit and healthy.

Every day you need to have:

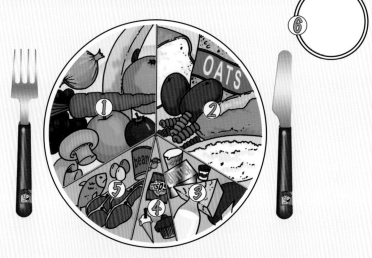

① Lots of FRUIT and VEGETABLES

② Plenty of BREAD, CEREAL, RICE, PASTA and POTATOES

③ Some MILK or DAIRY PRODUCTS

④ Not so many FATTY or SUGARY foods

⑤ Some PROTEIN FOODS such as meat, fish, eggs, nuts, beans or pulses

⑥ Plenty of water

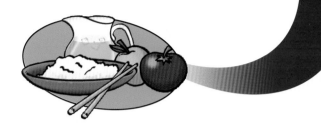

'Gimme Five'
FIVE A DAY portion information

- Aim for at least five portions of a variety of fruit and vegetables every day.

- Fresh, frozen, chilled, canned, 100% juice, and dried fruit and vegetables all count.

Here are some examples of portions which could make up your five a day target.

 2 satsumas

 3 tablespoons of peas

 A slice of melon

 A cereal bowl of salad

 1 medium banana

Healthy Eating

You don't need to eat for two, but you do need a balanced diet.

IRON

Green leafy vegetables, lean meat, dried fruit & nuts contain **IRON**. Not enough iron and you are likely to get very tired and may suffer from anaemia.

CALCIUM

Dairy products, fish with edible bones like sardines, bread, nuts and green vegetables are rich in **CALCIUM**, which is vital for making bones and teeth.

VITAMIN C

Citrus fruit, tomatoes, broccoli, blackcurrants and potatoes are good sources of **VITAMIN C**, which you need to help you absorb iron.

VITAMIN D

Margarine, oily fish and taramasalata contain **VITAMIN D** to keep your bones healthy and provide your baby with **VITAMIN D**. **Ask your doctor if you need to take a VITAMIN D SUPPLEMENT.**

FOLIC ACID

You will need extra **FOLIC ACID** from the time you start trying to conceive until the 12th week of pregnancy to help prevent birth defects such as spina bifida.
Take a 400 microgram FOLIC ACID tablet every day.

Healthy Eating

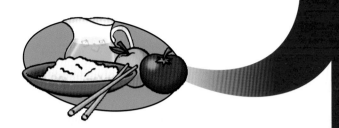

Foods to avoid during pregnancy

● Raw or soft eggs

● All types of paté and mould-ripened soft cheese

● Green top milk

● Liver or liver products

● Undercooked meat or poultry

● Unwashed fruit and vegetables

● Peanuts and food containing peanut products

● Shark, marlin and swordfish

● Excessive quantities of alcohol.
Drink no more than 1 or 2 'units' of alcohol once or twice a week. ONE UNIT IS:

 or **or**

¹/₂ pint of ordinary strength beer, lager or cider

A single measure of spirit (whisky, gin, bacardi, vodka, etc.)

A small (125ml) glass of wine (9% ABV)

Healthy Eating

● Breast feeding is the best way to feed your new baby.

● Breast milk provides perfect nutrition. It also protects your baby from a variety of infections and other illnesses, and reduces the likelihood of childhood obesity.

● Breast feeding reduces the risk of breast and ovarian cancer for mum and helps the womb to return to normal.

● Breast milk or infant formula provide all the food and drink your baby needs for the first six months.

● You can express milk if you want someone else to feed your baby.

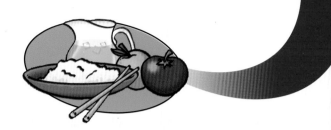

EXPRESSED MILK

● Can be kept in the fridge for up to 24 hours.

● Never reheat expressed bottles in the microwave as this can cause dangerous hot spots that could burn your baby's mouth.

● If you are using infant formula milk or you express breast milk it is essential to

WASH,   **RINSE**   and   **STERILISE**

all bottles thoroughly.

Healthy Eating

● If you are using infant formula it needs to be made up fresh for each feed, as storing made up formula milk may increase the chance of your baby becoming ill.

● Feeds should be made with boiled water that has been left to cool for no more than half an hour.

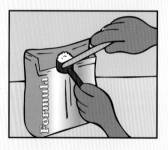

● Always follow the instructions on making feeds carefully.

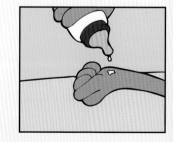

● If the milk is too hot, cool the bottle under the cold tap, but make sure the teat is covered.

● If you require a feed for later, keep boiling water in a sealed flask,so that you can make up fresh formula when it is needed, or use a ready-to-feed formula.

Healthy Eating

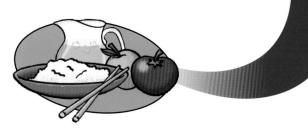

● Make sure you and your baby are relaxed and comfortable so that feeding time is enjoyable for both of you.

● Never leave a baby to feed alone from a propped up bottle.

● Throw away any unused milk immediately after use.

Oral Hygiene

Babies need healthy mouths - they use them to drink, eat, speak, cry and smile.

Good oral hygiene from birth sets the pattern for healthy teeth later.

● Breast milk is best for your baby.

BREAST IS BEST

It's easier, cheaper and healthier for baby and mum.

Oral Hygiene

- Sterilise all bottles and dummies.

- DON'T put juice into bottles.

- DON'T dip dummies into any food or drinks.

- Introduce a feeding cup at **six** months.
  Aim to stop using bottles and dummies by twelve months as this helps to improve speech development and prevent tooth decay.

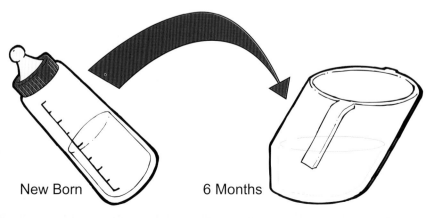

New Born   6 Months

Keeping Active

Exercise and fitness is important for you and your baby.

FOR BABY

At first your baby will spend a lot of time sleeping, but during waking hours will be keen to learn how to move his or her body.

● Give your baby chance to kick and explore his new world.

● Why not try baby massage to give you more confidence in handling your baby?

Keeping Active

● FOR YOU

It's really important to make time for you. A healthy active Mum is much more able to look after her baby well.

Don't forget all those post-natal exercises, especially for the pelvic floor.

● TOGETHER

Taking your baby for a walk in the pram is great for you both.

Try and make time for a walk every day.

Early Learning

DO

- Talk to your baby right from the start.
  Every time is talking time.

- Baby likes to hear your voice and see a smiling face.

Early Learning

DO

Hold your baby

Cuddle your baby

Play with your baby

Massage your baby

Early Learning

DO

● Let baby hear all kinds of noises

● Noise-makers are good toys

● Baby enjoys hearing you copy his noises

DON'T

- Shout at your baby

- Handle your baby roughly

- Shake your baby

- Hit your baby

Call your health visitor or GP if you have any concerns about your baby and don't know what to do.

Contacts

In case of an **accident, emergency** or just **advice** these ar
some useful numbers to ring for information and help.

NHS Direct 0845 4647

Your call will automatically be put through to your nearest centre
will be charged at local rates (may be more from a mobile).
www.nhsdirect.nhs.uk

Your local Health Visitor can be contacted via your GP practice.

Add your GP's number here

Your local Fire Service can be contacted for advice on fire preven

Child Accident Prevention Trust (CAPT) 020 7608 3828
A charity committed to reducing childhood injury.
www.capt.org.uk

First Aid Courses
British Red Cross 0845 608 6888
St John Ambulance 0870 010 4950

Useful numbers in your area: